AH, SWEET DANCER

Margot Ruddock

Ah, Sweet Dancer

W. B. YEATS
MARGOT RUDDOCK

A Correspondence Edited by
ROGER McHUGH

MACMILLAN
GILL AND MACMILLAN

Published by
MACMILLAN AND CO LTD
London and Basingstoke
Associated companies in New York Toronto
Dublin Melbourne Johannesburg & Madras

Printed in Great Britain by
WESTERN PRINTING SERVICES LTD
Bristol

CONTENTS

LIST OF ILLUSTRATIONS

ACKNOWLEDGEMENTS

My thanks are due in the first instance to the Yeats estate and to Mrs Simone Halliday and Commander Michael Collis; also to Mr Donal Donnelly, who first put me on the track of these letters. I am grateful to Professor Horst Frenz, Professor A. Norman Jeffares, Dr Mokashi-Punekar, Mrs Mrinalini Chitale for their advice; to Mr Richard Garnett and Mr Kevin Crossley-Holland for their assistance in preparing this book for publication; and to Sir Frederick Ashton, Mrs Robert Cathcart, Mr Douglas Cleverdon, Mr Valentin Iremonger, Mr Raymond Mander, Mr Robert Medley, Mr Tony Meneses, Mr Harry Partch, Dame Marie Rambert and the staff of the National Library of Ireland for help of various kinds.

R. McH.

INTRODUCTION

W. B. Yeats was sixty-nine and Margot Ruddock twenty-seven when they first met. Ruddock was her maiden name, but she had married, while still in her teens, a Cambridge friend of her brother's called Jack Collis, by whom she had a son, Michael, before they were divorced, her husband retaining custody of the child. Subsequently her career as an actress brought her in contact with her second husband, Raymond Lovell, while both were playing in the Terence Byron company at Bradford. They were married there in May 1932, and she retained Margot Collis as her stage name. She seems to have had considerable means at this time, for in 1933 she and her husband leased the Grand Theatre, Southampton, and the Theatre Royal, Bournemouth, for a year. This repertory venture proved a financial failure, resulting in a loss of some three thousand pounds. On 19 February 1934 their daughter, Simone, was born in Barcelona, and soon afterwards Raymond Lovell had his first real success as an actor in London.[1] His wife continued to act after her daughter's birth and developed the idea of creating a poet's theatre there. This brought her to seek Yeats's help in September 1934.

Yeats at this time had just passed through a period of prose writing and of political interest, somewhat barren of poetic

---

[1] This was in *The Queen Who Kept Her Head*, in which he acted Henry VIII, a role which he later played with equal success in *The Rose Without a Thorn*. He afterwards had many important parts in films, appearing in *The Man in Grey*, *Alibi*, *49th Parallel*, *Caesar and Cleopatra*, *Pickwick Papers* and others. His favourite part was Dr Johnson. He was elected a Fellow of the Royal Society of Arts in 1949, and he died in 1953.

composition, and had returned with new vigour to poetry. He himself attributed this to the Steinach rejuvenation operation of April 1934, of which he wrote later that it had revived his creative literary power and sexual desire. In his book of memoirs, *Since Fifty*, Sir William Rothenstein gives a good verbal picture of him: 'now in his later years, brown-skinned under his white hair, his dark eyes aslant, broad-shouldered and ample of form – he, once so pale and lanky'.

In the latter part of the year Yeats was writing his 'Supernatural Songs' and rewriting *The King of the Great Clock Tower* in verse. He had also revived his old wish to unite poetry with song and had begun a series of broadsides written to traditional airs. He had long disliked the predominance of realistic drama at the Abbey Theatre and so found the idea of helping a poetic theatre in London attractive.

When he first met Margot Ruddock in London, he saw a woman 'of distinguished beauty of face and limb'. Contemporary photographs of her bear him out. A notable feature of her beauty, as Yeats's poem 'Margot' indicates, was her eyes. She had, moreover, a lovely contralto voice. He thought that she had the potentialities of a great actress: 'there was something hard, tight, screwed-up in her', he wrote; 'but were that dissolved by success she might be a great actress, for she possessed a quality rare upon the stage or, if found there, left unemployed – intellectual passion'.[1]

He saw also that she might make an excellent speaker of his own verse; although handicapped by professional mannerisms, she improved under rehearsal by his friend Edmund Dulac and by Frederick Ashton,[2] to whom he brought her after hearing

[1] Introduction to *The Lemon Tree* by Margot Ruddock (1937).

[2] Sir Frederick recalls being asked by Yeats to rehearse Margot Ruddock in speaking verse in spite of the fact that he used to criticise the poet's own reading of his poems, 'rather impertinently', as he now considers. He was much struck by Margot Ruddock's looks and felt that she had 'definite potential as an actress but had obviously never fallen into the right hands',

her recite. When Ashley Dukes offered the use of the Mercury Theatre, which he had opened the previous year, Yeats formed a committee consisting of these three men, with T. S. Eliot, Rupert Doone of the Group Theatre, Margot Ruddock and himself.

He also introduced her to other friends, of whom Shri Purohit Swami, the Indian philosopher, poet and teacher, figures most prominently in these letters. Yeats had known him for three years and had written introductions to his autobiography, *An Indian Monk*, and to *The Holy Mountain*, the Swami's translation of an account by his Master, Bhagwān Shri Hamsa, of his travels in the Himalayas. Yeats at that time, according to one Indian commentator had 'accepted Indian life fully and with a fanaticism even Indians are not used to'.[1] During that year of 1934 the Swami had certainly influenced his 'Supernatural Songs' and Yeats had resolved to go to India to assist him in translating the Upanishads, a project eventually completed in 1936 in Majorca, where Margot Ruddock saw the Swami, under sad circumstances, for the last time. In his introduction to *An Indian Monk*, Yeats describes him: 'A man of fifty, broken in health by the austerities of his religious life; he must have been a stalwart man and he is still handsome.' Oliver St John Gogarty's description of him at Majorca is characteristically different: 'The Yogi, dressed in bright pink and looking like a bright carnation, sat with his hands folded on his ample paunch.' At any rate, when Margot Ruddock first knew him the Swami was fifty-two and had become something of a celebrity in London where he had founded and was lecturing at the Institute of Indian Mysticism. The few letters from him to Margot Ruddock which are among her papers are courteous and kindly and show a high regard for her.

---

though he found her very intense and she seemed 'a lost soul'. 'Yeats,' he writes, 'was obviously very taken with her.'
   [1] *The Later Phase in the Development of W. B. Yeats* by S. Mokashi-Punekar (Karnatak University, Dharwar, 1966).

It was in 1964 that Mr Donal Donnelly first mentioned to me the existence of Yeats's letters to Margot Ruddock. This led me to seek out Mrs Simone Halliday, her daughter, who kindly allowed me to make photostatic copies of them. When I sent these to Mrs Yeats, she wrote to say that, while she did not think that they should appear during the Yeats centenary year, she intended that they should be published eventually '*with her letters to WBY* and her own account of the Barcelona episode'. She added that the letters should not be censored or cut in any way. A year or two later, not long before her death, she sent me Margot Ruddock's letters to Yeats, together with many of her poems and other material referred to in this edition. There was a notable gap in the correspondence; no letters from Margot Ruddock to Yeats during the eleven months after their first meeting were included, although it is clear from his letters to her during the same period that she wrote several. Mrs Yeats subsequently verified that the missing letters are not among Yeats's papers and suggested that they might have been lost or destroyed during Yeats's stay in Majorca.

Their absence means that from 3 September 1934 to 15 September 1935 the correspondence runs one way, from Yeats to Margot Ruddock; from then until January 1936 the balance is fairly even; then Yeats's illness and his work with the Swami tilt it the other way during the first four and a half months of 1936; and after Margot Ruddock's visit to Majorca in mid-May of the same year this imbalance continues, though for different reasons. In all, thirty-one of these letters were written by Yeats, thirty-six by Margot Ruddock. One from the latter group has been included more appropriately in Appendix B.

Fundamentally the letters tell their own story of an intimate human relationship which if it 'was not without its fineness', as Yeats put it, was not lacking in touches of comedy, in grimmer realities and, towards the end, in tragedy. Since the friendship was based not only on mutual attraction but also on shared artistic and intellectual interests, the correspondence is also revealing on these matters. Yeats's advice about the technique of poetry, his criticism and emendations of her poems, his recollection of changes in his own poetic style, his views of the proper speaking of verse, of the use of refrains, of the arrangement of his own poems for recital add something to an understanding of his later work. We also see him faced with certain problems during the compilation in 1935 of that highly controversial anthology, *The Oxford Book of Modern Verse*; his difficulty in overcoming his prejudice against the Eliot–Auden school, which I think he never really surmounted, although it is notable that he also missed many of the qualities of Gerard Manley Hopkins's poetry; and also the problem of favouring his friends, including Margot Ruddock, Dorothy Wellesley and the Swami, all of whom are represented in the anthology, while, to take but one notable Irish example, Austin Clarke is not. At the same time it is clear that Yeats learned a great deal more about new trends in modern poetry during its compilation.

Besides telling us a little more about his later plays, notably *A Full Moon in March* and *The Herne's Egg*, Yeats's letters refer to several matters of peripheral theatrical interest; the heated controversy between Gordon Craig and other eminent men of the theatre in Rome in 1934, the Dublin reactions to the first Abbey Theatre production of O'Casey's play *The Silver Tassie*, the lasting bitterness of the early break with the Fays, as well as practical problems of 'Theatre business, management of men' during his last years as a Director of the Abbey.

If several of Margot Ruddock's letters borrow a reflected light from Yeats there are some which have flashes of insight, like her best poems, or show that generosity of spirit, that sensitivity to human suffering which Yeats admired in her. Something of her merits and limitations as a poet emerge from her letters and are exemplified more fully in the appendices. The letters also show a gradual recession of control and a growing diversification of effort, as the tide of circumstance rose around her. Indeed Yeats's remark in his introduction to her book of poems *The Lemon Tree* that the excitement of mysticism, the constant nourisher of his own poetry, was for her a 'perilous excitement' is reminiscent of Jung's comparison of Joyce and his daughter Lucia to two people going to the bottom of a river, one diving, the other falling.[1]

We know from the letters that Yeats wrote *A Full Moon in March* with a speaking part for the Queen so that Margot Ruddock might act it, and that the first song in that play was partly addressed to her. The lines

> Should old Pythagoras fall in love
> Little may he boast thereof . . .
> Open wide those gleaming eyes . . .

fit into the context of the letters. Yeats also shared her hope that she would play Decima (whom he thought she resembled) in *The Player Queen*, but this aim was frustrated both in Dublin and in London, to his annoyance.

Three of his last poems bear her image. 'At Barcelona', which he prefixed to her book, appeared under another title in *Last Poems*, which also contained 'Sweet Dancer'. The earliest of the three, 'Margot', was not included, was perhaps deliberately suppressed by him, and as far as I am aware is now published, with Yeats's account of how it was composed, for the first time.

[1] See *James Joyce* by Richard Ellmann (Oxford University Press, 1959) 692.

The difficulties of editing letters by Yeats have been admirably set out by Allan Wade in *The Letters of W. B. Yeats* (pages 16–18). In general I have followed his methods, correcting spelling or punctuation where this was necessary to clarity, retaining some slips where they seemed to fit in with the mood or stress of either writer. I have indicated where dates are conjectural or uncertain and have corrected them when they are definitely incorrect. Margot Ruddock's 'Almost I Tasted Ecstasy' follows all the idiosyncrasies of its original appearance in *The Lemon Tree*, and I have left the punctuation of her letters almost as it stood.

ROGER McHUGH

THE LETTERS

1

Riversdale, Willbrook, Rathfarnham, Dublin
September 3 [1934]

Dear Miss Collis,

Yes, I am sometimes in London, but often months pass before I go there, and then I am there for but a few days. I will try not to lose your letter, and if I do not I will let you know or let you know if I can. Even in London I have sometimes a vacant hour for a fellow artist, but at others business and fatigue consume my time. I thank you for your praise. Yours,

W. B. Yeats

2

September 24 [1934]   Riversdale

Dear Miss Collis,

I shall go to London on October 3 and ring you up before 11 on the morning of October 4. With the exception of a doctor I must see (nothing serious) I shall not tell anybody of my arrival until we have arranged our meeting – indeed perhaps not then. As a poet I am a solitary man, though I live in a crowd – one word of yours pierced that solitude. You spoke of the 'trueness' of my work, if you had said its 'veracity' or used any other word, such as reviewers use, it would have meant nothing. The fact that you found this word, your own word, made me see you, it was as though I saw your face. I do not want compliments but I want to know what people are like. I wanted to be sure, I wanted you to say just what you have said in your latest letter, that is why I asked whether you preferred my early or my latest work. I wanted to find your 'trueness' in your discovery of mine. Do not think that I await our meeting with indifference. Shall I disappoint you or shall I add to the number of my friends?

I had just such a project as that you describe, but circumstances have compelled me to create a realistic and folk theatre, where poetical and dance plays find their brief acceptance amid often rough satirical comedy. I do not leave here until October 3 because a new play about Parnell now has to be produced, in its performance perhaps revised.[1]

We shall ask each other questions, perhaps; perhaps I shall put a book into your hand and ask your to read out some poems, that too one of the ways to knowledge. When I was young I think I wanted to be deceived, but now I want wisdom always or as much as my blind heart permits. Yours,

W. B. Yeats

3

October 5 [1934]   Savile Club, 69 Brook Street, W.1.

My dear Margot,

I have asked Bumpus to send you *An Indian Monk* by Shri Purohit Swami. If it attracts you I will give you an introduction to its author. He will stay on in London for a year or so and a group of people have gathered round him, some are or were

[1] *Parnell of Avondale* by W. R. Fearon was produced at the Abbey Theatre on 1 October 1934.

members of the Theosophical Society, they study under his guidance. He is a well-bred, simple man, an Indian 'gentleman'.

I am tired, tired as if I had written all day yesterday—that is why my handwriting is so bad.

Thank you about Seymour Street. I have taken a little self-contained flat there and pay little more than half what I do here. I have taken it for a week from October 17. I have long wanted such a place. You are bound to nothing, not even to come and look at me.

Never be swept away into anything; live in self-possession, wisdom –

> 'Be secret and exult
> For of all things known
> That is most difficult.'

Did not Job call the way of wisdom 'the path of the eagle, that eye hath not seen'? I have got the quotation wrong, I think, I have not read it since I was a child.[1] Yours always,

W. B. Yeats

The way of wisdom is our own way, not the way of our ancestors, who throng in our blood, not the way found by some act of submission to a church or a passion, to anybody or anything who would take from us the burden of ourselves, that burden that is our glory – the way we as Europeans today must be everybody everywhere.

The Indian submits to a god, but that god is himself – every self.

I cannot spell today.

[1] Possibly Job 39: 26–7: 'Doth the hawk fly by thy wisdom, and stretch her wings toward the south? Doth the eagle mount up at thy command, and make her nest on high?'

In October 1934 Yeats attended the Fourth Congress of the Alessandro Volta Foundation in Rome, where he lectured on the Irish national theatre. The participants included Gordon Craig, Ellen Terry's son. The German architect he mentions was probably Professor Adolf Linnebach of Munich; 'Tairolf' was Alexander Yakovlevich Tairov, founder of the Kameny Theatre; while Filippo Marinetti was the founder of Futurism, which stressed the beauty of the machine age. 'Maeterlinck's little bit' may refer to the actress Georgette Leblanc.

4

Albergo Palazzo & Ambasciatori, Roma
Thursday [11 October 1934]

My dear Margot:

I reach London on 17th of October, my wife stays on and then goes straight to Ireland, keep me the eighteenth if you can. I shall ring you up at 11.

Here is my journal continued. Yesterday, Wednesday, Ashley Dukes[1] having an engagement for lunch – damn that man – I asked Gordon Craig to lunch, we are old friends, he has his mother's charm, her beautiful voice. At lunch he said 'if you ever want designers write to me for them' meaning that he would still work for nothing for me. He is the great man of the conference, all the young actors and producers gather round him. In the afternoon he started no end of a row. A famous German theatrical architect had just described his latest invention, a stage that rolls and winds and turns in every possibly way, when Craig rose: 'A producer who works for that theatre must know all that so and so knows, and so and so, and when

---

[1] Theatrical producer, playwright and translator of plays, married to Marie Rambert. He founded the Mercury Theatre, London, in 1933.

he knows all that his art will be dead; and when art is dead the nation is dead. I want men of 25 in the theatre', after that came uproar. Then Tairolf, a famous Russian producer, speaking with great passion said 'it is time to get rid of machines'. Then an Italian, Marinetti, defended them, an incredible orator. His hands went round and round in mid-air as though he were turning a wheel, and faster and faster as his passion demanded. Then another orator with equal passion denounced the machine, then everybody shouted, while the helpless chairman, Dukes, rang his bell. So on for an hour. When we were going home we had to stand in the hall waiting for taxis (it was raining) and there in the hall the row started again.

I am rewriting *The King of the Great Clock Tower* giving the Queen a speaking part, that you may act it. I have so arranged it that you can give place to a dancer (quite easy as you will both wear masks).[1] The old version of the play is bad because abstract and incoherent. This version is poignant and simple – lyrical dialogue all simple. It takes years to get my plays right.

I had some talk with Maeterlinck's little bit, found her intelligent and friendly – she has good English but her appearance is incredible.

O my dear, my mind is so busy with your future and perhaps you will reject all my plans – my calculation is that, as you are a trained actress, a lovely sense of rhythm will make you a noble speaker of verse – a singer and sayer. You will read certain poems to me, I have no doubt of the result, and October 19 I begin the practical work. Yours affectionately,

W. B. Yeats

[1] The prose version of *The King of the Great Clock Tower* had been produced at the Abbey Theatre on 30 July 1934; this rewritten poetic version was published as *A Full Moon in March* (Macmillan, 1935); the volume also contained another poetic version under the original title, in which the Queen does not speak.

5

Savile Club

Tuesday [postcard, postmarked 30 October 1934]

My dear Margot,

No, come at 3. A lunch that begins at 1 must leave off at
2.30 or so, but wait if I am not here. I cannot bear the thought
of a half-hour lost. Packing is so complicated and long and –
and – and – Besides – Yours,

W. B. Y.

6

November 13 [1934]   Kildare Street Club, Dublin c. 17

My dearest,

Tell me about Sunday night, about the Eliot dance play?[1]
I expected from an horoscope a postponement to Easter. It is
as well for it will leave December to us. I wonder if you would
think out the singing or speaking of (say) half a dozen of my
poems. I shall probably bring over a zither that we use at the
Abbey with Dulac's music. I will be able perhaps to introduce
you as a 'sayer' of my verse before the play begins. The B.B.C.
might help. Half a dozen poems in a studied order, with variety
and climax.

I have in my head two poems 'for Margot' but I may not
write them yet. A long toil on the play has tired me and I
want the rest of practical work or of a change to prose. I must

[1] *The Rock*, a pageant with dances, written for performance at Sadler's
Wells Theatre, 28 May–9 June 1934.

24

not meet you again a tired man. However the play opens with
a song partly addressed to you.

I

Every loutish lad in love
Thinks his wisdom great enough
(What cares love for this and that?)
All the town to set astare
As though Pythagoras wandered there
(Crown of gold or dung of swine).

II

Should old Pythagoras fall in love
Little may he boast thereof
(What cares love for this and that?)
Days go by in foolishness
But O how great the sweetness is
(Crown of gold or dung of swine).

III

Open wide those gleaming eyes
That can make the loutish wise
(What cares love for this and that?)
Make a leader of the schools
Thank the Lord all men are fools
(Crown of gold or dung of swine).[1]

Crown of gold, etc., prepares for something in the play.

I shall not comment on the word 'intrigue', but I have looked
it up in a French dictionary (I forgot to do it this morning).
The *English* word is certainly not an alternative to 'no word at
all'.

[1] Except for some minor changes, this is the first song in *A Full Moon
in March*.

I must wind up my letter. Lennox Robinson and Peak and Bowl or Boule — I think that is how they write their names, which sound like something very improper out of *The Golden Bough* — our new producer and designer, arrive in a few minutes to decide on our next production.[1] They obliterated the offence of their *Macbeth* by a magnificent performance of *The School for Wives* last night, excellent in acting, magnificent in costume and scenery, costume and scenery were black and white throughout. I am greatly comforted, for I rammed them down the throat of my committee and after *Macbeth* I thought my instinct had failed me. In all that has to do with human beings I am a gambler. I chose Lennox Robinson as manager before we had exchanged sentences by the shape of his back. How did you and I choose each other? I think even before we had seen each other's faces. Yours always,

W. B. Y.

Write an occasional letter to me at Riversdale, Rathfarnham, Dublin. My wife knows that we work on the theatre project. It is more natural if you write there.

7

Riversdale

Saturday [envelope postmarked 17 November 1934]

My dear Friend:

Until yesterday I was still correcting my dance play, but today I am free and I corrected one of your poems. I have added nothing, except what was necessary to get rid of some confused metaphors (For instance when you begin by 'O let

---

[1] Bladon Peake and James Bould came over from England, and their production of *Macbeth* opened on 25 October 1934. Molière's *The School for Wives* opened on 12 November.

me glide' it causes confusion to write a little later 'sweep on no tide' etc.) and to take out 'the poppied sheaves' which are a worn-out metaphor. You always have passion, that is to say the substance of all art, but you want a greater technical precision, a greater mastery of deliberately chosen detail.

I think that I agree with your husband that a lot of people could have made up 'for fun' something better than Eliot's poem, but I want Eliot for the Mercury because he represents a movement that has grown all over the world and is strong at the Universities. It seeks modernness in language and metaphor and helps us to get rid of what Rossetti called 'soulless self-reflections of man's skill' but it does throw out the baby with the bath-water.

I have looked up the word 'intrigue' in the French dictionary and I find that it means among other things 'to puzzle, to perplex'. We shall probably do that in any case without taking pains in the matter. I think our work will throw us much together, that is if you do not weary of me, fame will link our names for the work's sake, and doubtless, to use a phrase of George Moore, people 'will hope for the best'. 'I always hope for the best,' he said when I accused him of spreading scandal about a certain cousin of his and a well-known public man.

The last paragraph of your letter which came this morning, has made me happy. The belief 'that there is nothing new' outside one's self is the beginning of all great artistic creation.

A Californian musician called a few days ago and is coming again tomorrow.[1] He is working on the relation between words and music. He has made and is making other musical

[1] Harry Partch (b. Oakland, California, 1901) who was then studying the history of intonation at the British Museum on a Carnegie grant. He invented many new instruments, formulated a 43-tone scale and described his theories in *Genesis of a Music* (University of Wisconsin Press, 1949). Many of his works were performed in the United States, 1942–62, among them *Oedipus*, a music drama (Mills College, Oakland, 1952). See also Appendix C, page 133.

instruments which do not go beyond the range of the speaking voice but within that range make a music possible which employs very minute intervals. He speaks (does not sing or chant) to this instrument. He only introduces melody when he sings vowels without any relation to words. I hope to bring to London with me the zither we use with Dulac's music, and you might try this method of getting variety. He has been given a fellowship by an American institution to create these instruments and to make musical settings for my *King Oedipus*. I shall give him an introduction to Dulac. We cannot however use him in our work at present, he is on his way to Spain to perfect his discovery; it is still, I think, immature. He is very young, and very simple.

O my dear I would like to go on writing, for I have much to say, but I spent most of the morning on that poem of yours and I must stop. I have publishers' agreements to read through and sign, and then I go my periodical long walk with a certain Irish poet whose scandalous narrative vein delights me. He is writing a play more or less like Burns's *Jolly Beggars* for my theatre.[1] Yours with all affection,

W. B. Y.

O find me that intricate coverlet
Where Innocence lies asleep, or let me glide
Without complaining to tranquillity:
O may I drift to death and never wake
Even to summer, even to budding leaves,
Even to God, even to love with thee.

No, no, I would not waken for a world
Of flutes and fiddles nor for that great bowl
Of different joys that fuse into a mass

[1] F. R. Higgins, whose *Deuce of Jacks* was produced at the Abbey Theatre on 9 September 1935.

And fill the throat with nauseous delight,
Nor for those harsher joys that are love's pin
Scratch the heart raw and burrow through the thin
Shell of the spirit. I drift upon some tide
From all those treacheries; I am set free,
I shall lie down and hide
In that elaborate easy bridal bed
Where Innocence waits for me.

I have asked Macmillan to send you my new book.[1] Do not
bother about those long essays. Read *Resurrection*.

8

November 23 [1934]   Riversdale

My dear:

I hope your depression is but the result of your cold. Some
days ago I got a strong feeling that I ought to be in London
(perhaps but my wish to be there) but on looking up dates
found that I should have to return for today, when 'The Irish
Academy of Letters' committee meets (and without me might
lack a quorum), then there are other things to be done up till
December 5. Before I go to London I have to decide if the
producer and stage decorator, engaged to control our 'second
company', are to go on after Xmas. I shall judge by their production in a few days of *Six Characters in Search of an Author*.[2]
I have written to Miss O'Dea for a room for December 6. If she
is full I shall go to the Quebec Hotel till I find some cheaper

---

[1] *Wheels and Butterflies*, published that day.
[2] Pirandello's play was produced at the Abbey Theatre on 3 December
1934.

place. I see your image always before me, that image of kindness, sweetness, beauty. Should you have to go on tour London will have no charm for me though some other city may have.

In the list of poems, which you are working at, I notice two in which I dramatise myself as a man, 'Broken Dreams', 'May God be thanked for Woman'. You should as far as possible select poems where a woman speaks or where it is not clear whether the speaker is man or woman. If you speak as a man, your woman's charm will weaken your effect, as it would were you to play a man's part on the stage. Your voice will always be the voice of woman, I think, even if you make it very impersonal. Only the members of the Papal choir could be both man and woman and in our humanitarian age have lost this privilege. Arrange say half a dozen lyrics in an order to give you variety and contrast and climax. You might begin with 'I am of Ireland', then give a couple of lyrics in which there is no singing, then 'The Old Men Admiring Themselves in the Water' then 'Leda and the Swan'.

Here is a suggested list. (I have not my book at hand and so take the titles from your letter.)

(1) 'I am of Ireland'.
(2) 'O cruel death give three things back'.
(3) 'What lively lad most pleasured me'.
(4) 'The Old Men Admiring Themselves'.
(5) 'Leda and the Swan'.

I would like you to look at a poem (not to learn it) called, I think, 'Crazy Jane Reproved' because after each stanza I write 'fol de rol, fol de rol'. I think when you find words like that in an old ballad, they are meant to be sung to a melody, as Partch the Californian musician I told you of sings his 'meaningless words'. He uses them to break the monotony of monotone. There is no special value in 'fol de rol', any meaningless words would do. Kingsley once used 'barrum, barrum, barrum, baree'.[1] I have asked Dulac to report upon him. If he approves of his music, I may send him to you if he is still in London (He too longs for Spain and plans to finish his work there). I put 'fol de rol' at the end of the stanzas in this poem to make it less didactic, gayer, more clearly a song. If you feel inclined to you may put such words at the end of any stanza of any poem where there is not already a burden.

I will write later about your poems. God be with you my love,

W. B. Y.

The list of poems I give is mere suggestion. You could for instance substitute for (2) or (3) 'Running to Paradise' without so losing variety or climax. Something sung, not spoken, before 'Leda' is, I think, essential.

9

November 26 [?27], 1934   Kildare Street Club

My dear,

I wronged Miss O'Dea, she writes that I can have my old room – she had waited to find out if it would be vacant. I am half sorry I was enquiring about service flats. I shall go to Seymour Street for a fortnight at any rate.

Here is a first poem for Margot. I wrote the first verse on Sunday but could get no further. I knew I was too excited to sleep and took a sleeping draught. I got up in utter black gloom, 'perhaps after all' I thought 'this nervous inhibition has not left me' – I pictured Margot unsatisfied and lost. How could I

[1] Refrain of Charles Kingsley's 'Last Poem' (*Collected Poems*, Macmillan, 1880).

31

finish the poem? How could I finish anything? My wife saw my gloom without knowing its cause and made an appointment for me for last evening with Ireland's chief wit Gogarty. I was not to see him until 9 so I got a private humourist of my own discovery to dine at the club. From 7 until 12 I listened to Rabelaisian stories of the Dublin slums – wild tales more wildly told. Then most of Monday I worked on the poem and only got the second verse. Dreading gloom I invited yet another guest to dine, a lame ex-British officer and Free-State general.[1] His wounds had given him my inhibition and several others. He had cured himself by Oriental meditations. Every morning he stands before his mirror and commands himself to become more positive, more masculine, more independent of the feelings of others. Six months ago he was ordered off the hunting field by a political enemy. He turned his horse and rode the man down. If he goes on with those meditations he will be murdered. His hobby is Asia and North Africa. Hour by hour he told me astonishing stories of North African Negroes. Then I went to bed and went on with the poem and finished it a little before dawn. I will not know for some months whether it is good or even if it runs smoothly. What your public house and your glass of ale is to you wild stories are to me. They are my mind's chief rest. Without them I should go mad.

That poem of yours had wonderful phrases, when you wrote 'split and splayed apart' when you made that use of 'splintered bone' you were a great poet.[2] I tried to disengage these lines from a confusion created by lack of practice. If you cannot get such poems right let us invent a pseudonym or collaborate in half a dozen poems. I think they would live.

Ah my dear I forgot to say when I commented on that word 'intrigue' that you are of course at liberty to tell any intimate

[1] Captain Dermot Macmanus.
[2] See Appendix A, page 120, for her poem, in which only the first of these phrases appears.

friend you can trust, but we will discuss all those things next week.

I have read *The Times*, the *Morning Post*, the *Daily Mail*, the *Evening Standard* reviews of *For Ever* and I cannot tell from their reviews how it went.[1] Was your husband able to play? How is your own cold?

The post is going. Yours,

W. B. Y.

MARGOT

I

All famine struck sat I, and then
Those generous eyes on mine were cast,
Sat like other agèd men
Dumfoundered,[2] gazing on a past
That appeared constructed of
Lost opportunities to love.

II

O how can I that interest hold?
What offer to attentive eyes?
Mind grows young and body old;
When half closed her eye-lid lies
A sort of hidden glory shall
About these stooping shoulders fall.

[1] Noel Langley's play, *For ever*, based on the story of Dante and Beatrice opened at the Shaftesbury Theatre on 26 November 1934 and ran for only just over a month. Raymond Lovell had the small part of Geri del Bello. The first reviews appeared on 27 November, so Yeats must have misdated his letter.

[2] In the manuscript Yeats wrote 'Dumfounded' and then struck it out and substituted 'Dumfoundered'.

33

The Age of Miracles renew,
Let me be loved as though still young
Or let me fancy that it's true,
When my brief final years are gone
You shall have time to turn away
And cram those open eyes with day.

The gap between the previous and the following letter is due to the fact that Yeats was in London in December 1934. Wade (page 830) gives a letter to Dulac, conjecturally dated 10 December 1934, which begins 'Margot and I will dine with you tomorrow' and says also 'I will discuss your suggested programme with Margot'.

10

Wednesday [January 1935]   Riversdale

My dear Margot:

I have a congested left lung. I am more or less convalescent, but it is a slow business and I have little power of concentration. I have just begun to sit at the fire for a few minutes each day.

I will send you a copy of *The Full Moon in March* for Rupert Doone;[1] I will ask Macmillan to send him *Wheels and Butterflies* as he may prefer *Fighting the Waves* (a producer's play which I could abandon to him as I could not *The Full*

---

[1] Rupert Doone (born Ernest Reginald Woodfield) began his career as a dancer and was associated with the Diaghilev Company, becoming its 'premier danseur' shortly before Diaghilev's death. In 1932 he founded the Group Theatre Company, and was responsible for the first productions of Eliot's *Sweeney Agonistes*, Auden's *The Dance of Death*, the Auden–Isherwood plays, and works by Spender and MacNeice. In 1935 he was beginning an important season at the Westminster Theatre.

Moon in March where I can permit little modification of the stage-directions). *The Resurrection* and *The Player Queen* have been decided upon once and for all, but I think the third play could still be changed and reviewers to my surprise have constantly picked *The Fighting of the Waves*. I will write to him about it in a day or two.

I miss you very much; when I was tired looking at you we could always quarrel. (I have a quite new scandalous story about a certain acquaintance of mine that would serve to start the old theme.)

I shall dislike swallows for the rest of my life unless they fly in crowds.

I cannot write yet about the poem. Yours affectionately,

W. B. Yeats

Write here and as you will, there will be no accidental opening.

11

February 25 [1835]   Riversdale

My dear Margot,

I have not written for some days because I have been correcting proof sheets – the first work I have been permitted. When I am on my feet again – if a crisis in the Abbey Theatre permits – I may go to England to pay a couple of country visits and to see you. I am trying to understand for the sake of my *Cambridge* [sic] *Book of Modern Verse* the Auden, Eliot school. I do not mean to give it a great deal of space, but must define my objections to it, and I cannot know this till I see clearly what quality it has [that has] made it delight young Cambridge and young Oxford. When you and I have argued it out my mind may clear. By the by what my wife said of Edna [St] Vincent Millay was 'all hot lobster and mountain tops', which is perhaps exactly what the youngest generation would say of my work if they did not think that I had lately excluded 'the hot lobsters' from the menu. *The Shadowy Waters* is perhaps very 'hot lobster'. Your friend never meant you to take him literally when he said that he would never have forgiven you had you altered one word, and that 'authenticity' was the one thing that mattered. He is a scholar and knows that the famous stanza in *The Ancient Mariner* about 'the ribbed sea-sand' was by Wordsworth.[1] All writers have given or accepted just such help. What matters is not what your friend seems to mean by 'authenticity' but quality – one more good poem. Kipling and I, though we have never met, wrote when very young men for a review edited by the poet W. E. Henley.[2] He rewrote us both – I never complained and never heard that Kipling did. I admit that some years later when he rewrote Henry James, 'The screams of Henry James', as a friend of mine said, 'filled the universe.'

Here is an episode from *The Arabian Nights* which amuses me. It might serve for a motto for a very advanced book upon the education of children. Scheherazade, the queen of story-tellers, says to her husband that she [is] about to tell certain anecdotes and that she must warn him that 'though these anecdotes are very moral they might seem licentious' to certain minds. 'Do not let that stop you,' says the King, but adds that perhaps they had better send away her little sister who is playing among the cushions; but Scheherazade says 'no', because 'There is nothing shameful in speaking of those things that lie below our waists.' My life is for the moment made up of such discoveries as I re-read Balzac and *The Arabian Nights*. When I

[1] Wordsworth wrote two lines, not the whole stanza, according to H. N. Coleridge.
[2] *The Scots Observer.*

36

lay down my book I watch the great tits, the blue tits and the tom-tits eating bread on the windowsill. The best Arabian nights, and even certain parts of Balzac have as little psychology as those birds, and that is why we never forget them. Perhaps I want to see your beauty again for no better reason than that which makes me like looking at the blue tits. Yours affectionately,

W. B. Yeats

The doctor tells me that it will be early April before I am completely recovered, but I think he exaggerates.

12

March 13 [1935]   Riversdale

Private
My dear Margot,
   I have had a letter from Ashley Dukes which I cannot understand. He wants to know if I think all production should be in the hands of Rupert Doone? He says that he does not think so. Now I had heard from Rupert Doone on March 5 (day before your committee meeting at the Mercury). He assumed that Tyrone Guthrie would produce *Player Queen*. I have written to Ashley Dukes to say that my work should not be produced by Doone but by a producer accustomed to 'romantic plays'.[1]
   I have a feeling from Ashley Dukes's letter that he has not told me all. That something has happened of which I knew nothing.

   [1] It is clear from a letter from T. S. Eliot to Rupert Doone of 20 March 1935 (now in the possession of Mr Robert Medley) that Doone had by then decided to take no part in the project, apparently because he was being asked to produce five plays and felt he would not have nearly enough time to do so.

What happened at the meeting at the Mercury on (presumably) March 6? You have not written about it nor has anybody else. Please write to me by return or I may make a mess of things.

I write in great haste. Yours affectionately,

W. B. Yeats

13

[Postcard]
March, 23, 1935   Kildare Street Club

My dear Margot,

I wonder if you could find out Tyrone Guthrie's address (if he is not in the telephone book). Your husband may know it. Probably Ashley Dukes would give it me; but it may be best to see Guthrie first. Yours always,

W. B. Yeats

14

[undated, probably late March 1935][1]   Riversdale

My dear Margot,

No we do not differ – we are at cross purposes. I am not criticising Edna [St] Vincent Millay (of whom I know nothing). I was amused by my wife's phrase because I thought it perfectly

[1] The theme of this letter follows closely on Letter 11, but 'I have sent the plays to Tyrone Guthrie' seems to imply that she had answered his request for Guthrie's address. Perhaps she did not answer Letters 11 and 12 until she received Letter 13.

expressed what Eliot, Doone, perhaps Dulac, think of romantic acting and poetry. As long as you are ready to take a word here and there I admit this obvious way may be the best way for you. You have the sense of rhythm, follow that and something will achieve itself. I hate Gerard Manley Hopkins, but people quite as good as I am admire him. He belongs to the movement immediately before mine (I knew him in Dublin and found him querulous and over sensitive to the movement that made diction artificial, oratorical, or ornamental).[1] His poetry and Meredith's – as somebody has pointed out – belong to each other; and my movement – I gave it its formula 'the natural words in the natural order' – was the escape from artificial diction. There are no rules only formulas whereby we escape from the sins of our forefathers. In all arts we select some virtue and make that chief. Make rhythm or 'hot lobster' your virtue – the Elizabethans were full of 'hot lobster' – and all will be well. I even admit that you may be right about my early poems in this sense – those early poems in their objective simplicity, their folk life, are greater in kind than my later poetry (which are better poems) but one has to take one's raw material from one's time, one's life. A day came when I could no longer live those simple poems – I had to face ceaseless popular insult in creating the Irish Theatre and I became bitter. I remember a woman commenting on the change in my face. Now that I am old and my work is finished I may have a few years to seek the sweetness I have lost.

I am worried. You do not say if you received the envelope of your typed poems I sent to you some days ago. I am most of the day here in my bedroom – when I sent the poems I had I think gone into the next room – a little library – for the first time – a great adventure. I have to depend on others to post my

[1] In a letter to T. Sturge Moore (12 July 1935) Yeats wrote: 'My period is from the death of Tennyson. This enables me to put Hopkins among the Victorians.'

letters – on my daughter or the gardener mostly. I marked the envelope to be 'registered'.

I enclose a copy of a letter from Vincent [Rupert] Doone, sent me by Miss Beauclerk. I have sent the plays to Tyrone Guthrie. If he accepts all is well. The contrast of the two schools should give us great publicity. I must be in London long before the plays begin – I may be able to get the press interested and I want to study the two schools of stage management. Yours affectionately,

W. B. Yeats

The production of The Player Queen *by Ashley Dukes did not take place as planned in the spring of 1935. In a letter to Olivia Shakespear (16 June 1935) Yeats alludes to 'false, fleeting per-jured Ashley' whose promise to produce it in September 1935 he regarded with disbelief.*

There is a gap of some four months between Letter 14 and Letter 15. Yeats was in London for a brief visit in April 1935, and stayed at Seymour Street, but he was not well and appears to have returned to Dublin as soon as some business affairs were settled. Although convalescent for some months thereafter, he visited London again in late May and early June 1935. Appar-ently he saw Margot Ruddock this time before being brought by Lady Ottoline Morrell to see Dorothy Wellesley at Penns in the Rocks, Sussex. He was interested in including some of her poems in The Oxford Book of Modern Verse. *On his return to Dublin, the selection of poems for this anthology and the correction of proofs of* A Vision *occupied his time; in addition the celebration of his seventieth birthday brought a flood of messages of con-gratulation which had to be answered.*

15

July 13 [1935]   Riversdale

Dear Margot,

Did I write to you yesterday? This question does not mean
that I am going mad, but that I have a way of completing a
letter in my head and thinking that I posted it. This illusion is
worst when I write many letters. Yesterday I wrote 17, and
today – it is 12.30 – I have already reached that number. If I
wrote to you yesterday I explained that these letters were in the
main letters of thanks to people who subscribed to the Rossetti
drawing given me at the birthday banquet.

I want typed copies of your recent poems. I have to decide,
my dear, whether I am to put you into *The Oxford Book of
Modern Verse*. I would like to take the opinion of one or
two friends. I like you too much to be a good judge. I think
you are good now, you certainly will be in a short time, but I
must not deceive myself or you. In any case I would like to get
you published in (say) the American review, *Poetry*.

What is happening to you and to your husband? Have you
forgiven me for my long silence? I could hardly help it, illness
reducing my working hours, and then that great mass of letters,
at first those that had come while I was ill in London.

I shall be in London for a day or two at end of August or
early September. I am taking my daughter (aged 16) on a
couple of country visits – John Masefield, Dorothy Wellesley.
The country visits over, I leave her at Stratford for the Shakespeare festival and go to London. Yours affectionately,

                                              W. B. Yeats

Am I to put you in *The Oxford Book of Modern Verse?* I
do not know. I am leaving out famous men. Perhaps I will

delay my decision till I have all the material before me. My anthology should be the standard anthology for some time.

16

My dear Margot,

Thanks – I can use two, perhaps three of the poems. Keep to those tight metres. I am sure of the 'O Holy Water, Love I Learn' and I think of 'Sea Shell' and 'I take thee Life.' I like least 'Sea Urchin' and 'Child for these undying dreams, etc.'[1] Those long lines make you oratorical and vague (never call any poor wretch a 'maiden' that word is as dead as 'swain'). I believe that I am making the standard anthology and it is very exacting work. I understand what you feel about the word 'love'. I too hate that word and have I think avoided it. It is a name for the ephemeral charm of desire – desire for its own sake I do not think that it is because I have grown old, that I value something more like friendship because founded on common interest, and think sexual pleasure an accessory, a needful one where it is possible. Paris and Helen were Romantic Love, and both were probably fools; Odysseus returning to Penelope through ten years' heroic toil (though frequently unfaithful on the way), Penelope's patient waiting, was the classical ideal of man's and woman's wisdom. Both had Ithaca to think of.

It was good of you to offer to meet me at the boat. But it is not necessary. I cross over in a couple of days and my daughter comes with me and, after a couple of hours' rest, go to Lady

[1] The first and third of these poems were included in *The Oxford Book of Modern Verse*. See Appendix A, pages 120–2.

Gerald Wellesley's house in Sussex; on August the 21 we return to London, my daughter goes to Stratford for the Shakespeare festival and I stay a few days in London. I shall probably stay at the Savile that I may be looked after.

I am still ill – if I can avoid any effort that puts me out of breath, or any chill for a few months, I should be as vigorous as ever. That is why I am going to Majorca. The doctors urge it upon me. Then too I want to be as much alone as possible that I may write poetry again. Yours affectionately,

W. B. Yeats

The next letter refers to the row over the Abbey Theatre's production of O'Casey's The Silver Tassie. *Its rejection by the Abbey in 1928 had led to an estrangement between O'Casey and Yeats, who took the initiative in ending it in 1934, during O'Casey's visit to Dublin. The Abbey Theatre produced the play on 12 August 1935, and it ran for a week. Yeats attended the first night with his wife and daughter. The offending director was John Weldon, 1890–1963, who wrote and directed under the name of Brinsley MacNamara. He was a considerable playwright, whose 'satirical novel',* The Valley of Squinting Windows, *had been published in 1918 by Maunsel. He was one of the founder members of the Irish Academy of Letters in 1932. For an account of the controversy see David Krause's* Sean O'Casey: The Man and his Work *(1962) which, however, neglects to mention the public support which heartened Yeats.*

17

My dear Margot,

I will send *Full Moon in March* with this. It is packed away somewhere. Send it to Nancy Price[1] or give it.

Yes, no need to think any more about Ashley Dukes except as a swamp we got mired in.

No, I have not yet attacked the Lord Mayor, or even found out if I must.[2] Something else turned up. When I reached Dublin priests were preaching against the Abbey Theatre, and clerical newspapers denouncing it because of *The Silver Tassie*. We were used to that, but the major event was that a director appointed six months ago joined the attack, and said publicly that he would resign if we ever did the play again. This man (his name is MacNamara) was in a panic. Twenty years ago he wrote a satirical novel and had to escape from his father's house through the back door while the mob was breaking the windows in front. He set out for Dublin covered with straw in a farmer's cart. His one passion now is to have the mob on his side. My problem was to get rid of him in such a way that he could not be a martyr for religion. He had published in an interview what had taken place at our board. I got a resolution passed censuring him for 'breach of confidence', asked [for] his resignation and said if I did not get it in a week I would have him expelled. It came last Friday. He has really given us a great advertisement. The Abbey has not been so prosperous for years – every seat sold. I have been very polite, no man was ever stabbed more courteously – poor devil.

[1] Actress and producer, who founded the People's National Theatre Company in 1933.

[2] Possibly because of his support for the Irish censorship, see Letter 26, page 57.

Try and get them to put on my plays in October – I might then be able to see them – I go to Majorca on November 1, and that is as late as I dare put it.

I am coming to the end of my work on the anthology. I find it exciting.

I am longing for your poems. Your symbolism is new yet traditional. Certain writers, Milton for instance, repeat some old legend that there was once nothing but spring and autumn and that the heat of summer and the cold of winter came at the Fall. You reverse, passing from the fever-heat to the cold of winter. Make your symbolism complete, denounce spring as well as autumn. It is the heroic doctrine.

Good-bye for now my dear – I have a longish letter about the anthology to write. Yours,

W. B. Yeats

I cannot read that sentence about the garden that seems to read 'There was a Kive in the garden I don't know why'. What is a 'Kive'?

Your letter of Saturday has just come. Sorry about Nancy Price and delay.

Who translated your Plotinus? There is one consummate translator, Stephen MacKenna,[1] but he is very expensive.

---

[1] MacKenna, who was a friend of Yeats and Synge, had been associated with the Irish Literary Revival. Yeats apparently was unaware that he had died in London in 1934. His edition of Plotinus, Yeats believed, confirmed many of his own ideas in *A Vision*.

18

My dear Margot,

I send a revised copy of *The Full Moon in March*. If you look at it you will find it better dramatically. It makes the play turn on stronger hinges. Only a few words are changed however. The bit where she is told that a woman conceived from a drop of blood is much more actable – you may be asked to play it.

I have been working at the play all morning and now I must rest. Some people are coming on business – partly theatre.

Learned last night that the man who has been attacking *The Silver Tassie* with most energy has neither read nor seen the play.[1] He wrote to a friend of mine to borrow a copy that he might get material for a new attack. He has probably never bought a book in his life. This all very dull, forgive me. It is the sort of thing that fills my time.

Please, my dear, send back the other copy of play. My wife's careful mind covets it. Yours,

W. B. Yeats

The next is the first extant letter from Margot Ruddock to Yeats. Through him she had met Shri Purohit Swami, who was a prolific composer and singer of songs in his native dialect. A volume entitled The Song of Silence *by Shri Purohit Swami was published by Chitale (Poona City, undated). It contains over one hundred verses, some rhymed, some unrhymed, in English. Among Margot Ruddock's papers are some typed prose-poems of a similar nature,*

---

[1] Probably P. T. McGinley, President of the Gaelic League, who wrote over the pseudonym Cu Uladh.

headed 'Songs of Silence'. They are not in the volume mentioned and are probably attempts at translating some other verses of his. This would explain her interest in Tagore, whom Yeats had helped to revise his translations into English for Gitanjali *(1912) to which Yeats wrote an introduction.*

19

15/9/'35   14c Westbourne Gardens, W.2., Bayswater 5091

Darling Yeats,

I have sent the last version of the play to Nancy Price, and had a letter from her secretary saying she was out of town for a few days, but that they would forward it on.

I am sending back the other to you. Which poems of Tagore did you do – all?

I am doing the Swami's without rhythm. Cannot finish my own. 'Like the year.' The first verse I cannot do. No beginning and no end. Perhaps that's an idea! I will think it out.

Raymond has taken to crossword puzzles as he has no work.[1] He hopes to win a prize. I too hope he does soon!

This is a little poem I wrote.

> O milk of peace
> That flows
> From the Earth's breast
> Who drinks thee knows
> No thirst

---

[1] 1935 was a low point in his acting career, and for the next two years he was often struggling to find work. Thereafter many good parts came his way.

O chance, O Breath
Of fate
O mighty wind
Who blows with thee shall find
His path

O Body, thou
Deserted pleasure ground
None seek
To pleasure who have found
Satiety

[unsigned]

20

Telephone
Booking Office   4450
Secretary's Office   4341

ABBEY THEATRE
DUBLIN C.8.

Date,

Directors W. B. YEATS, WALTER STARKIE,
LENNOX ROBINSON, DR. RICHARD HAYES,
ERNEST BLYTHE, ~~BRINSLEY MACNAMARA,~~
F. R. HIGGINS.
Secretaries ERIC GORMAN, T. J. ROBINSON.

Tuesday [17 September 1935]

My dear Margot,
      The crossing out of a name signifies that we have got rid of

the objecting director. He sits in public houses, hoping that some old friend may speak to him or associates with pietistic journalists who are the dullest company imaginable.[1] The theatre continues packed.

Did you know that Speaight made a muddle that day – Nancy Price's party was at 5.30.

Your little poem is a theme, a good theme, but not yet a poem. I think you should write in rhyme and use regular stanzas for the present. I cannot make out your last verse. 'O Body' is clear but what is the next word? Then comes 'Deserted pleasure ground' then a line I cannot read; then comes I think 'To pleasure who have found Satiety'. These unrhymed lyrics look easy and are very difficult. You must give something else instead of rhyme. There will be few examples in my anthology. The very difficulty of rhyme will make you go deeper into yourself.

I went through all the poems in *Gitanjali* and *The Gardener*, changing the rhythm when it lacked and finding better words, constantly going to Tagore for a more literal translation.

I like your Tibetan Tale – the saint would be [a] fine stage character, if, when he came out of his cavern, his nettle-like hair could sting.

I am utterly absorbed in the anthology, finding wonderful things – poetry has become philosophical and profound in the last ten years, not the well-known poems but poems ignored by the press. I have learned now a great deal about rhythms. But of all things we will talk if I go to London in October, and that

[1] In a letter of 25 September 1935, Yeats told Dorothy Wellesley:
We are accepting into our friendship (but not our theatre) the man we put out. Higgins said to my wife, 'I cannot quarrel with the man. I like the way he looks at a glass of porter, a long look, a delicate look, as though he noticed its colour and the light on it.'
[2] *Gitanjali* was published with an introduction by Yeats in 1912; *The Gardener* appeared in 1913.

depends upon Nancy Price. Should I write to her, do you think? I prefer to leave her to you, my dear. Yours,

W. B. Yeats

The Full Moon in March will be published in book form early this autumn.

Traces of the bitterness caused by an old split in the Abbey Theatre are evident in the next letter. W. G. Fay and his brother, Frank Fay, had been associated with the Irish Dramatic Movement from 1901–2. In 1908 serious differences of opinion between W. G. Fay and the directors about the Abbey Theatre's artistic and management policy had led to the resignation of the Fays. Accusations of dishonesty were made by both sides. For the Fay's viewpoint see the book referred to in this letter: The Fays of the Abbey Theatre *by W. G. Fay (London, Rich and Cowan, 1935):* also The Abbey Theatre *by Gerard Fay (Dublin, Clonmore and Reynolds, 1958).*

21

September 20 [1935]   Riversdale

Private
My dear Margot,

You wired to the theatre yesterday to know if Fay was alive and working. I wrote that he was, but promised fuller information.

Fay was a charming comedian when he left us. I think he must have failed as [an] actor because his voice was not strong enough for large theatres. I do not want him to produce any play of mine, *first* because I do not think he would be natural with me and *secondly* because he is not sufficiently educated to produce work of my kind, *thirdly* because he had, and probably has, the temper of the devil and is a black intriguer into the bargain. He left us because the best part of our company resigned. He may be a changed man, now that his ambitions are gone, but I do not want to risk it.

Of course you may want him for something else altogether. Apart from production and management I have found him a charming actor and a most amusing talker.

I hear well of his production of recent years, but it has I think been confined to amateurs in some amateur shows.

I have not seen his book but have seen reviews. It seems good.

I am in a rush of work, my dear, I have four committee meetings this afternoon and a business matter to settle with somebody at lunch. Yours,

W. B. Yeats

22

September 24 [1935]   Riversdale

My dear Margot,

Here is the only photograph I have. I paid for it so, if it is used for press, there is no fee payable to the photographer. Let me know what is happening.

If Nancy Price wants to do *The King of the Great Clock Tower* tell her I have a version of it in verse but following the prose closely. I can send her this in proof.

If she is going to do *Pot of Broth* (Fay excellent in it) tell her that one of the songs, 'Paistin Finn' is not quite right for the music. I will send her the correct version.

You represent me. Do what plays of mine *you* like or you *and she* like. Yours,

W. B. Yeats

When does Miss Price propose to rehearse? I shall, I suppose, be in Majorca.

Nancy Price went ahead with arrangements for the production of a 'Yeats Festival' at the Little Theatre, London. It was to consist of The Pot of Broth, The Hour-Glass *and* The Player Queen. The Player Queen *had been first produced by the London Stage Society at King's Hall, London in May 1919 and by the Abbey Theatre in December 1919. When Frank O'Connor became a director of the Abbey Theatre in 1935, he and Hugh Hunt wished to produce it with Jean Forbes-Robertson as Decima. 'But Yeats had promised the part to an actress with whom he was friendly at the time,' O'Connor recalled in his autobiography,* My Father's Son; *and when O'Connor refused to support this, 'all he would give us was* Deirdre'.

Meanwhile Nancy Price was also rehearsing The Hangman. *This was an adaptation by Pår Lindberg of a novel by Pår Lagerkvist and had been produced in Norway in March 1935. An English translation by Eric Maesterton and M. V. Harding was put on by Nancy Price's People's National Theatre Company at the Duke of York's Theatre, London on 22 October 1935. The cast included Frank Vosper, Marius Goring and Herbert Lomas. Margot Ruddock had the small part of the Boy's Mother in the medieval scenes. The original tale by Lagerkvist,* Bödeln (*1933*), *had an anti-violence theme born of his dislike of the Nazis.*

23

Sunday [13 October 1935]   14c Westbourne Gardens

Dear W. B. Y.,

We are still rehearsing for *The Hangman*. I have not heard when we start rehearsing for the plays yet, *The Hangman* opens tomorrow week I think, it needs a lot of rehearsing, it is almost as large a production as a musical comedy.

I hear that Ashley Dukes is doing the Becket play with Bobby Speaight in it on October 28th to be followed by your plays, it was in the paper a few days ago, but I have not heard anyone speak of this.

Raymond, after having three months out of work (an act of God to make him more careful with his money) has got a very good film coming off soon, and now it will be my job to extract enough (how I don't know because I cannot ask) to keep the family going for some time.

It is wonderful the way he accepts me now and listens – it is still difficult to get him to wash, I suppose it was just a spasm, I would not say this to anyone but you. I have not seen the Swami, I think he has perhaps gone away with a man he said might take him away for a little as he was ill.

I

Thought's a
Poison shoot
From a sick
Soul's root

2

Pure soul
Has no need
Of its flower
And seed

3

Soul is healed
When she
Can dissolve
To joy.

Knows all thought
Can learn,
(God's a word
Outworn).

Margot

THE SOUL'S CESSATION

She gives not
Nor yet witholds,
But as a
Ripe bud unfolds.

She, as peace breathed
From a flower
Is at last
Her own desire.

The next letter is incomplete and impossible to date exactly, but it must have been written before the 'Yeats Festival' opened on the evening of Sunday 27 October. The Little Theatre was then in the middle of a long run of Lady Precious Stream, *and the Yeats plays were given as matinees on Monday, Tuesday and Thursday, 28, 29 and 31 October. From her letter it seems that she may have played Decima (the Player Queen) on the last night only. But if so, Yeats seems to have been unaware of this when he wrote Letter 26. It seems possible that the missing part of the letter expressed despondency about her acting and some fear or illusion about sacrificing her little daughter, Simone, to her own apparently hazardous career as an actress. This would explain Yeats's desire to restore her confidence in Letter 25.*

24

. . . containing Nancy Price's.

If it hadn't been for Speaight I should not have got Decima
on the Thursday even.

Will you be at the Sunday performance? I want you to see
The Hangman too if you have time. This producer has the look
of being good, and an exciting play about good and evil.

Will write again soon, love, Yours,

Margot

> All great Sorrow
> Should be sweet
> And Love *must* have
> Frozen feet.

Thank you for your letter this morning. All right only I think
I must have wrote it wrong, it is

> My *soul* is a seabird
> But we perch in the sea.

25

Thursday [17 October 1935]   Riversdale

Very Private
My dear Margot,

You cannot act because, absorbed in spiritual things you
have lost interest in the particulars of life. It does not help you

to think of Simone dead because you know she is not dead. Instead of thinking of her think of what I am going to tell you. Yesterday I had a lump cut out of my tongue, tomorrow I shall know if it is cancer. I had not meant to tell you but do so now, as it may help you to act. Yours affectionately,

W. B. Yeats

Remember that even a saint returns to life and its particulars, even a lyric poet must so return. Generality is our vice and we think it our virtue.

The operation referred to in Letter 25 seems to have been that which he mentioned in more guarded terms in a letter to Dorothy Wellesley of 13 October 1935; he said that it would take place on the following day, and he asked her to tell nobody about it, to safeguard against exaggerated reports.

On 24 October he had recovered and crossed via Liverpool to London, where he attended the Little Theatre production of The Player Queen *on 28 October. In at least three of the four performances Joan Maude played the Player Queen, Margot Ruddock the true Queen. Sir William Rothenstein recalled 'Yeats would have preferred the parts reversed; but I thought Joan Maude's interpretation of the character exquisite.' (Since Fifty.)*

26

October 29 [1935]   Savile Club

My Dear Margot,

I go to Sussex tomorrow morning and have been writing all day. Tonight I dine with Dulac.

You were magnificent yesterday. Whenever you went near

the lady who plays the Player Queen she, for all her beauty, faded out. You must hold on – you may become a great actress, a great artist, indeed with the right part you are that already. You have precision and passion.

If Miss Price's conscience awakes and decides that you are to be Player Queen please wire to me at once

c/o Lady Gerald Wellesley

Penns in the Rocks

Withyham

Sussex

Yours always,

W. B. Yeats

P.S. The typed script has come. No you did not send the wrong script to Nancy Price.

I have changed my tactics about the Lord Mayor. Yesterday the *Irish Times* started on the theme and continued it today.[1] I supplied the material. I found it impossible to attend to anything – head full of all this poetry I am reading so I must keep the peace till my head clears.

God be with you.

[1] There is no reference to Yeats in the *Irish Times* of 28 October. On the 26th it had referred to a discussion on censorship planned by P.E.N. for November 1935. The implication is that Yeats intended to undermine the support given to censorship by the Lord Mayor, Alderman Alfred Byrne. On the 29th the *Irish Times* mentioned Dr John Larchet's music for *The Cat and the Moon*, *The Dreaming of the Bones* and *The Land of Heart's Desire*. His music for the third play, it noted, had been heard publicly for the first time at the P.E.N. dinner to Yeats in June 1935.

27

11/11/35   14c Westbourne Gardens

Darling Yeats,

Ashley Dukes rang up to say he could not back me in my project although he thought it was a good idea, I am now sure I have done with the stage, I told the Swami, he is not quite sure till he has tried so he asked someone he knows, but I am sure I have done with it as far as becoming anything big on the stage is concerned.

I am writing so much, Swami told me he got all his poems from Meditation, I think of him all the time, here are some.

LOVE SONG

In solitude
My silent guest
I lay my soul
Upon Thy breast

Here she finds love
Without despair
Peace, without pain
At parting here,

Shy with the sweetness
Of such joy
She doth common
Day employ

Wean my heart
Of all but God
Until it
Is purified

And then, when
My heart is free
I will give
It back to Thee.

Though to think
Rejoiceth me
Love I will
Not think of Thee,

Though thy heart's
My resting place
Yet I will
Not seek embrace,

Not till soul
Has shed her pain
Will I come
To Thee again.

This I have rewritten[1] but I want to post this letter now, I shall not sleep all tonight.

I love you darling.

Margot

AUTUMN CRYSTAL EYE[2]

O Thou living self
Cast to flesh
Out of my dead heart
Born afresh

---

[1] The first five verses, originally written in a separate column on the left, have been struck through.

[2] This poem was eventually reduced to two stanzas (the fifth and sixth) and appeared under the same title in *The Oxford Book of Modern Verse*.

Into a deep strange
Burning youth
As the year to change
Seeking truth.

Like a ragged child
Forlorn spring
Checked Thee by the hand
Lost, weeping

Summer's fiery breath
Drowsed thee deep
In her wanton arms
Held to sleep

Autumn crystal eye
Look on me,
Passion chilled am I
Like to Thee,

Seeking sterner truth
Even now
Longing for the white
Frozen bough

Icy streams of peace
Running clear,
Winter of the soul
Sweet to bear

As the year defies
Winter's lash
Slipping from the seasons
I from flesh

Light with its own strength
Soul shall wing
And no Summer beckon
And no Spring.

28

Friday, 15th November [1935]   14c Westbourne Gardens

Darling Yeats,
    Thanks so much for your letter, I have written three little
songs with the music, as well.

> Child shut not
> Your heart away,
> Though to love
> Shall bring Thee tears
> Tears will bring
> My love to Thee
> Weep, O child
> For love of me.
>
> Love, let me weep
> For Thee and me
> A single tear
> Of pure love shed
> To melt the heart
> Of God.

I have written a melody for this, it's rather nice but I am not
much good at the Theory of Music.

Lord let me hear Thy voice
Though silence blest
Hush hearts to sleep
Who in Thy silence, weep.

When these get more religious if you approve of them I want them to be Swami's 'Songs of Silence'.

Margot

By the end of November 1935 Yeats's work on The Oxford Book of Modern Verse *was finished and he had arranged to leave public life and theatre business behind and to sail to Majorca for the winter, partly for reasons of health and partly to work with Shri Purohit Swami on the translation of the Upanishads. The next letter was addressed to him there. Margot Ruddock had been in Majorca and in Barcelona the previous year.*

29

Nov. 30/35   14c Westbourne Gardens

Darling Yeats,

I am not quite sure of the date of your arrival, whether 4th or 7th, so am writing this to await you.

Here are a few songs, one I have set to music, and am going to try to get it published in the spring when the Anthology comes out. *Summer Feast.* I have an idea of trying to get hold of the rights of a book called *The Gadfly* by a man called Voynich, to make into a film story.[1]

[1] *The Gadfly* was published in 1895; its author, Mrs E. L. Voynich, was an Irishwoman married to a Russian anti-Czarist. It had been dramatised in New York in 1899 and was filmed by the Russians in 1955. It had an enormous success in Russia both before and after the Revolution, over

It is the most marvellous book I have ever read, but out of print now, and I am scrounging round for a second-hand copy. For years I thought of it as a play.

But I am afraid it will have to be wrapped up for the censor, about a Cardinal who has a child, and finally becomes a very high power in State affairs, the child grows up embittered because the father brought him up to believe he was his pupil, not his child, and finally leads a Revolution against the Cardinal, who captures him. And has to choose between letting him off, which he says he will do if *his* son will promise to give up his revolutionary cause, or having him shot.

The Son will not give up, and they have a marvellous scene in the prison. Then he is taken out to be shot, but he is so beloved that everyone aims to miss, and with wounds all over him he laughs at them, and finally the Cardinal steps out and finishes him off. Then the last scene is in the Cathedral with everyone gathered round to listen. And he denounces his Cardinalship, and breaks forth like a madman, saying he's sorry he ever had anything to do with the church at all. And falls dead crying for his son.

The two men's parts are marvellous, and a woman I could play, Gemma. The dialogue is beautiful. If I can get hold of the book I know a man who will cut it.

A friend of mine, a Mrs Durlacher, an old lady of about seventy may be in Majorca. I told her about you and the Swami going there, she is very intelligent, and may turn up. Thank you so much for the book *Full Moon in March* and the poems in it. Also for your last letter and advice about the lyrics. I am trying it. The play sounds very exciting. Darling I love you so much, I wish I was with you in Majorca.

---

four million copies being sold. The Soviet cosmonauts Yuri Gagarin and Valentina Tereshkova both testified to the Gadfly's influence on their personal lives. See Lewis Bernhardt, 'The Gadfly in Russia', *Princeton University Library Chronicle*, XXVIII, no. 1, Autumn 1966.

By the way if you ever want injections or anything, my doctor in Barcelona was, KELLNER, CALLE MALLORCA, BARCELONA. Love,

Margot

While in Majorca, in addition to collaborating with the Swami on the Upanishads, Yeats was working on his play The Herne's Egg. *The idea of the play was taken from Samuel Ferguson's epic poem* Congal (1872), *but Yeats's treatment of it was influenced by the Swami. In a letter to Dorothy Wellesley, dated December 1935, Yeats wrote: 'Shri Purohit Swami is with me and the play is his philosophy in a fable, or mine confirmed by him.'*

30

Hotel Terramar, San Agustin, Palma de Mallorca, Espana
Christmas Day 1935

My Dear Margot,

I like 'Quiet', the third verse is fine.[1] I wonder is the last right. It is not a contrast to 'Cold Harlot Night'. Do you not want a contrasting warmth, not a diminution? Does not the logic of metaphor require that dawn brings the opposite of 'Cold Harlot Night'? I like greatly 'Process'.[2]

I am glad you are to go back to the stage. One can neither think nor do anything right until one gets the material foundations in their place. If you've good luck your genius will grow and you will become independent. You will never lose what you have gained in these last two years. Act constantly, act anywhere, so that you act. I think you have the rudiments of a

[1] See Appendix A, page 122 for the published text.
[2] See Appendix A, page 123.

64

W. B. Yeats at the microphone
Taken on the occasion of his broadcast 'My Own Poetry' of 3 July 1937,
in which Margot Ruddock spoke one of the poems

W. B. Yeats and Shri Purohit Swami in Majorca

great actress, but it will be hard for you precisely because you have no facile commonplace gift, like that of the girl who played my Player Queen at the Little Theatre. I wish I could have seen more of your acting, it would have helped me to write the strange play I am now writing. My heroine, a holy woman, is raped by seven men, and the next day calls upon the heavens to testify that she has never lain in any arms but those of her god. Heaven thunders three times, and the men who have raped her fall upon their knees. This is but one episode in a wild fantastic humorous, half-earnest play, my first full-length play.

I am full of imaginative life, but my heart is behaving badly still – four-day storm in the voyage out when I had to hold on to this object or that, upset it.

Swami and I are translating the Upanishads together – we are both to put our names on the title-page. Here is a sentence I like: 'Mere preachers and soldiers are his food, death its condiment; how then can a common man understand Him.'

Here is another:

'They have put a golden stopper in the neck of truth; pull it Lord; I am full of longing; let out reality.'

Weather here is warm and still – sun shining, sea blue. My window is wide open. Yours affectionately,

W. B. Yeats

31

14c Westbourne Gardens
Saturday (I think) [28 December 1935]

Darling Yeats,

I have had *much* to drink, for I have been at my play *all* day and all the *days*, it doesn't matter, one speaks the truth when one is drunk in spite of things said to the contrary.

I am very excited about my play, and I am excited because I think it might be rather good, and if I could repay all you have done by writing one single thing good I would be happy. Therefore I *am very* excited and even if it comes to nothing I will have been excited and possibly have excited you about it. I am going to send the first act, it has only two acts, four scenes, one in first, three in second so the first act will be longer than normal. It might not be literature, but it will get off my chest what I want to say – *up till now* it is never what one wants that happens so I don't suppose it will ever be produced or that I shall be in it but still it is written *because* of you and that's that.

Margot

There is a poem of Housman's that goes:

> 'If truth in hearts that perish
> Could rend the powers on high
> I think the love I bear you
> Should make you not to die.'[1]

They say he is a bad poet, I disagree.

32

New Year's Eve /'35   14c Westbourne Gardens

Darling Yeats,

I think *The Immortals* is not good for a title so have changed it to *Into the Sun* either that or *Before Morning*; it is getting very exciting, and the Philosopher has turned into you, but I am

[1] The first verse of *A Shropshire Lad*, XXXIII.

nearly mad for I have no quiet to work and have to snatch bits here and there with Molly[1] and the baby flitting in and out, and Raymond and his friend Wilfred Stevens waving to and fro, I wish to God I lived alone in a garret for six weeks or so to get the thing going properly.

It is terrible not to be able to find responsible people to look after one's baby, I really don't know how people get along, no mother seems to be as tied as I am, yet Molly made a pudding with turkey dripping in it the other day and gave it to the baby, it upset her for days, and I daren't leave here with Molly now, or ever go away, but she is getting married soon so I may get rid of her, however it is no use making plans, they always fall through.

The second act is very immoral, but I hope, bracing. I am an actress. The whole of the second half of the play is duologue, do you think it matters? There didn't seem to be anyone else to come in. Love for now,

Margot

33

January 6 [1936]   Hotel Terramar

My dear Margot,

I cannot judge whether you are right to finish with duologue alone without reading the play or its scenario. I am very sorry for your trouble over the child, etc. Acting may be the solution, as it should give you enough money to hire a proper nurse – it seems the only immediate way of getting the foundations of your life firmly fixed and yourself independent.

Here it is warm sun, my window is wide open, the sun

[1] Described in Letter 55 as 'my Irish maid for whom I thank God'.

streaming in. I have finished the first act, or first scene of my humorous serious faery tale, and the Swami's and my translation of the Upanishads (it will appear over both names) goes on rapidly. Yours always,

W. B. Yeats

34

Thursday, 9/1/36   14c Westbourne Gardens

Darling Yeats,

Thanks so much for your letter and glad you are all right. I have received a book of poems of 'Michael Field', thank you ever so much, they are lovely.[1] I could never have believed women wrote them. I like 'Bury Her at Even' best.

Here are a couple of mine.

The play is going on, it has now less duologue, as more people have come into it, a couple of old ladies, an artist and his wife, a postman and a Sanitary Inspector. So it's got nine important people now – two who don't say much.

I have taken a room for next week for 7s just to type during the day because there is no quiet and I drive Raymond mad with the typewriter. So shall do all I can in a week. Have got the whole thing rough now. Molly is getting married on Sunday. Perhaps she'll be better when she is not so vacant. As I'm very vacant thinking of other things it makes it impossible to get anything done in the house.

Raymond has no job and we are sued on all sides, but it doesn't worry me in the very least. Lovely not to care what

---

[1] *A Selection from the Poems of Michael Field*, published with a preface by T. Sturge Moore (The Poetry Bookshop, 1923). 'Michael Field' was the pseudonym of Catherine Bradley and Edith Cooper.

happens. No sign of work. I think I must finish this play for some reason, I don't know why, then shall attack my Theatrical Manager friend. Love,

Margot

Yeats had an attack about mid-January 1936. He wrote about it in similar terms to Dorothy Wellesley on January 19 and to Margot Ruddock in Letter 35, which presumably was written about the same date.

35

[c. 19 January 1936]   Hotel Terramar

My dear Margot,

I have been ill. My breathing became both difficult and painful. I sent for a very clever old Spanish doctor. He cut off all writing until the pains had gone and then stopped creative work (I can go on with my work with Swami). I have been resting a great deal and writing hardly any letters. Today I am much better owing to a good night – indeed lack of sleep is my main trouble. I sleep best bolt upright. The doctor sees no reason why I should not be normal in a few weeks especially as he seems to have found the root of the trouble and certainly climate and place are as perfect as possible. I spend much time sitting in the sun on a terrace by the sea.

I hope they sent you the right 'Michael Field' selections by Sturge Moore with introduction by him. 'Michael Field' wrote nothing lasting until a few years before her death when probably under the influence of Charles Ricketts, a fine mind and man of great knowledge, she wrote a few lyrics very classical in form. It would not harm you to imitate her, there are some models that can be copied without loss. I like your last little poem, but you cannot go on always with the same form.

Did you get *Seven Days of the Sun* by Turner, and what do you think of it if you did? I like the section called 'Thursday'.[1]

Do write and tell me these things.

I have had to stop my play but I will take it up again when I am better. Before the doctor intervened I had written Act 1 and Scene 1 Act 2, and a lyric which I like. Yours affectionately,

W. B. Yeats

36

14c Westbourne Gardens
Monday, Jan. 2 1936 [date incomplete – 2 January was not a Monday – probably 20 January]

Darling Yeats,

I am sorry you are ill, I had a feeling you were as a matter of fact one evening about ten days or a fortnight ago. I hope you will be much better soon.

I am writing absolutely different stuff now but it has no form. I find the little poems won't hold what I want to say. I shan't do any more.

I am writing a story called *Curtis YEAST*, the story of a farm boy who became a singer. A woman hears him singing in the yard, and takes him up. He doesn't want to leave the farm, he is quite happy really except for moments of terrific emotion. He says, 'But why should I want to be famous, I'm quite happy.' (He has a superb voice.) And she says, 'Because later if you don't make use of your talent you'll be unhappy always instead of only sometimes.' So he starts to have it trained and

[1] A long philosophical poem by W. J. Turner; Yeats included part of it in *The Oxford Book of Modern Verse*.

comes to London and hates it all so much. That's as far as I have got at the moment. They have typed the first act of my play. I will send it you all soon. It is finished. My new poems haven't form. I can't write in that form any more. I can't write tightly any more. I have studied the latter poems of 'Michael Field', the ones where they are dying of cancer.

I like the loose rhythm in them but rhythm is a thing I feel I must not copy. They are beautiful, those last ones, written I think after one of the 'fellows' was dead, and the other one dying of the same thing. One goes:

> Beloved, my glory in thee is not ceased,
> Whereas, as thou art waning, forests wane;
> Unmoved as by the victim is the priest,
> I pass the world's great altitudes of pain.
> But when the stars are gathered for a feast,
> Or shadows threaten on a radiant plain,
> Or many golden cornfields wave amain,
> Oh then, as one from a filled shuttle weaves,
> My Spirit grieves.

Poetry depresses me so much now, whereas it used to be a solace. There is something so sad in all great poetry, and yet I feel there should not be. Why? If we cannot be supremely happy eventually what is the use of everything. We might just as well be cats and dogs, and if we *can attain* supreme bliss *permanently* what is the use of sad poetry? Even if it transcends its own sadness, the sadness must have been there, therefore the poet must have been miserable and therefore I don't want to be a poet any more, name or no name. Write and tell me if you are better or not or I shall suddenly appear. Sweet I love you.

Margot

P.S. I like Saturday best of *Seven Days of the Sun*. I liked it all though, a lovely vitriolic book.

37

Tuesday 28/1/36   14c Westbourne Gardens

Darling Yeats,

Here are two poems in my new fashion, or not as the case
may be.

It certainly gives one more scope for saying things and ables
one to write more strongly – but whether they are anything in
form I don't know, although I spent quite a time on them.

Everyone seems to have gone mad today about the King's
funeral. They've all left their homes and flocked to see the pro-
cession.

Raymond promised he'd rise at six this morning and go with
some friends to see it, but he did not.

I hope you are better.

Will send the play at the end of the week as soon as it gets
back from being typed. How are you, better I hope? Love,
                                                              Margot

*About 26 January Yeats had another attack. Among Margot
Ruddock's papers is a letter from Shri Purohit Swami dated 29
January which says: 'Today he is worse. The doctor does not
promise great hopes for him. I have wired to Mrs Yeats asking her
to come. Yeats is bearing himself with great courage; he knows the
inevitable is coming. What more can I say? You know what I
feel, and how strongly for him. If the worst comes you should not
be surprised; hence this letter.'*

On 31 January the Evening News *reported on the front page
that Yeats was 'gravely ill' and 'suffering from a heart attack',
and the* Evening Standard *in its Londoner's Diary that Yeats
was 'remaining in Majorca until he has recovered from his serious
illness'.*

38

Saturday evening [1 February 1936]

Darling Yeats,

On Friday morning at ten minutes to ten as I was on my way to my dairy to shop I had the most extraordinary experience. You definitely appeared in a sort of mental vision, and you got up from a bed. I stood quite still, it was so tremendous a thing. I shook all over, you looked and kept on looking at me. You went on for about five whole minutes, which is a very long time when thinking, and I made my way into the milk shop in a state of complete dream and didn't know what to buy!

I came back and told Raymond I was worried and then thought shall I wire him, then I thought no I won't, it may not mean anything – so I went out to tea with some people. When I returned Raymond came in with a newspaper and said, 'You were right about Yeats, he is seriously ill again.' I *had* to ring up, which I did, and the next morning I wired I was coming because I simply had to. Hope I didn't seem indiscreet. I wouldn't have done so for the world but for what had happened. I do hope you are better and will get better.

If you want me, and circumstances are such, I may come. Any time you wire I will come. If you don't, I am thinking of you just the same.

Margot

On 1 February, the Swami wrote to say that he had wired her not to come, as Yeats was out of danger and Mrs Yeats was arriving on 2 February: 'It was very kind of you to propose to come by plane': he wrote, 'and Dr Yeats understands the gesture more than anyone'. He added that Yeats and he had finished the Upanishads.

39

5.2.1936   Hotel Terramar

My dear Margot,

I have had your letter, describing your Friday morning
vision. Friday was a bad day with me – I was gasping for
breath. I am now quite clearly convalescent, and have the ease
of body and mind. My wife has arrived on Sunday and has
taken charge. The doctor tells me that I would be better than
I have been, when this attack is over. It was very good of you
to think of taking that long expense of journey, but fortunately
it was not necessary. I have a very good Spanish nurse and the
doctor who seems to know his business.

I imagine that we will carry out our original programme, and
my wife and I will stay here till the end of March, not venturing
back until the weather is warmer in Ireland and in England. I
have a good deal to say about the little poems you last sent me,
but I want to put it off until I am more vigorous.

I hope prospects are improving for you. Don't let the
Mercury Theatre forget you. I suppose *Murder in the Cathedral*
will sooner or later come to an end, and some new play go on
there.

                                   [signed] W. B. Yeats

40

9/2/36   14c Westbourne Gardens

Darling Yeats,

Here is a play, tell me what you think of it because I shall go by what I hear from you in deciding whether to try and get backing for it.

It is not literature, and therefore Ashley Dukes will not be interested. I do not particularly want him to be as I have been at great pains to write it about ordinary people, and so that people can understand it without being intellectual, what I want to know is do you think the interest will hold?

I don't think anyone will suspect the fantasy until the end do you? Or what will seem fantasy to them rather, I don't mind if you say you think it is rotten, but I depend upon your opinion before going all out for it, I have my own cast in mind, and should like to get backing and do it myself, with a producer of course, it must be played superbly, not overdone and not underdone. If you think it's any good I shall try for this, and put it on myself in a commercial theatre. There is a man I know who might back me, I have no assurance of this but would try if you think it worth while, if not I will keep it a secret.

Do not read it until you are well enough, there is no hurry. So glad to get your letter dictated to the Swami last night, and to know you are easier, not in pain.

Ann is the part I wrote for myself. Love always,

Margot

41

21/2/36   14c Westbourne Gardens

Darling Yeats,

I hope you are feeling a bit better now. I heard from the Swami you were having a pretty tough time of it. I have accepted a job for rep. twice nightly in May. I don't feel I want to do it, but nothing else seems to come my way.

Nothing I write seems any good and the plays are no good, nothing's any good I do. I wish I could get rid of this dreadful sense of the futility of being alive at all. I have been in bed with tonsillitis so perhaps that accounts for the depression. You once said Man gets happier and happier. I get steadily more and more miserable (perhaps you didn't include women!). Hurry up and get well and come to Crewe of all places and see me in plays that will bore us both intolerably! – We shall be doing one a week.

I could cut my throat from ear to ear cheerfully this evening if only I didn't hate the sight of knives and blood so much. And who knows but that I might have to go on doing twice nightly rep. for the rest of Eternity!

I shall go and get drunk, lucky to be able to do that too! Love,

Margot

42

14c Westbourne Gardens

[Undated, possibly late February 1936]

Darling Yeats,

> Giving all I have
> Yet shall all be mine
> I shall drink the Earth
> Like a vintage wine!

Here is a poem. The sun cheers me up and I am better and not so depressed. It was that awful fog I think. How are you? There is no news but that extraordinary things are happening in my head! Sometimes with regard to people.

I have a new mat in the sitting-room very bright colours – and it cheers me. All my love,

Margot

43

Darling Yeats,

The play I sent you is bloody, like a debate and all the people are mouthpieces not real people. I am writing another with more flesh and blood people, do not be bored with reading the other.

The man at Crewe has offered me three pounds less than I got before with him, and I have had a letter from Raymond's aunts for whom I have a regard in which they say, 'Do not think we are interfering, but isn't Simone very young to be left without a mother?' It is true, and it confirms my own feelings so strongly. After all if I can't write a bloody good play by sticking at it I might as well pack up. And working one's guts out in rep. for less than it costs one to live is stupid. I wouldn't mind if I was keen, but I'm not, it's too much, leading parts every week that don't interest one, I've done it all and I'm not going to again. One shouldn't go back in one's work – so I've written to say I don't think I'd go, told him about the aunts and the play I'm trying to write.

It's no use going up to Crewe and being worried about Simone when one rehearses 10–1 and plays 6–11 every day, and learns lines in the afternoon.

I saw my first husband today, he took me out to lunch and we went to see Charlie Chaplin's new film[1] – and that's all, said the March hare – and a great pity as far as I'm concerned because what's the use of having a nice body and wanting to give people happiness if no one will take it?

Really men are most extraordinary. You can go and practically offer to sleep with them, in fact one might almost say

[1] *Modern Times*, which had opened at the Tivoli on 11 February.

implore them to take one (not that I did so) and they won't so much as blink an eyelid with passion. Yet if you walk off and leave them they nearly die wanting you. I don't understand it all.

It's a dreadful thing to say, but apparently it's the same with God. Look how one has to trail in misery after it or him, or rather the Spirit of Man, which it is. I don't see why anyone should suffer for anyone at all, why can't we all be blacked out *if* we want to be – when I think that I have before me possibly forty years of life my spirit quails.

I am writing a very sad play. I think if you make a thing miserable enough people say it's good because it must be true. Whereas a year ago I could get fairly happy on two and a half pints, I cannot even get faintly drunk on that now. Don't let this letter depress you. I am really happiest when in the depths of misery because then nothing can be worse than it is – and if it goes right one misses the weight of things. Love,

Margot

44

4/4/36   14c Westbourne Gardens

Dear Yeats,

Those who love me have written this!

Is it your opinion as man to man that these with a few of my very young poems, those that have form, and those that have not and possibly one or two lyrics, I may yet write from ecstasy, would make one volume that will live? Love

Margot

There is no other copy at all.[1]

---

[1] Whatever was enclosed in this letter has not been preserved with it.

45

14c Westbourne Gardens

Dear Yeats,

I write this letter not knowing the result. I have been told
and written something. I do not know what. I send you the
voices because in answer to my agony of had I written enough
the voice said, 'Halve that which is done and it won't do.'
Earlier, with the few short poems came 'Yeats put English
poetry in its place through me' – a statement of fact, no
more.

I will not send more until I hear from you. Love,

                                                              Margot

Do not forgive those you want to be forgiven by.

*When convalescent, Yeats moved with his wife into a villa, the
Casa Pastor, about the beginning of April 1936. On 6 April, he
wrote to Dorothy Wellesley, describing the villa in similar terms
to those of Letter 46.*

46

                    Casa Pastor, San Agustin, Palma de Mallorca, Spain
[Undated: early April 1936]

My dear Margot,

I am now convalescent but shall, I gather, have to spend
about two months here in that pleasant state, so you will not
see [me] I think till early June. This house is on a hill and is
surrounded by a wide balcony where I sit and look out over the

sea. The house is not at all the house where your philosopher appeared, and this, I think, must have been an old farmhouse – there is one sitting-room divided by great marble pillars and purple curtains; there are white walls with mouldings and through the high windows, one sees the pilasters of the balcony and a great expanse of sea – a setting for a film. It is the summer villa of a Palma stockbroker, a very pleasant place, and one no more criticises the architecture than that of a bride's cake.

I have read the [play] carefully, and, though you will not get it taken, nor would it act before any audience I know, it is well constructed and well written. It will [not] act because your audience would find your thoughts too unfamiliar. Shaw can write a play where everybody is his mouthpiece because he takes the popular thought upon the stage, plays with it, and reverses it. You and I can only put our own thought there. Yet I do not think a play where everyone speaks my thought can be the greatest kind of play no matter how written. Goethe said, 'a philosopher needs all philosophy but must keep it out of his work' (which he could not do). Take some plot which seeks to express all in the action and where nothing is said about the action; do not speak through the characters, let them speak through you, and you will find that at some moment of crisis they will speak at once passionately and profoundly. This play, though not a good play, has greatly increased my admiration for [your] intellect and made me confident of your future. You have a gift for dialogue, for plot, for situation (how amusing that incident of a boy insisting in the midst of tragedy that they must take no baths). There is at least one lovely passage (page 5, last scene). It begins 'I always thought' and ends 'the Old one'. There [is] even a sense in which its failure delights me. I know from it you made your new philosophy part of your self, that you see life by its light instead of seeing it something re-mote, something outside life. If you can [see] life through your

Margot

all famine struck sat ?, & then
Those generous eyes on mine were cast,
Sat like other aged men
, gazing on a past
That appeared constituted of
Lost opportunities to love

II
O how can I that interest hold)?,
what offer to attentive eyes?
mind grows young and body old;
when has closed her eye-lid lies
A sort of hidden glory shed
about their stooping shoulders falls,

III
The age of miracles renew,
Let me be loved as though still young
Or let me fancy that its true,
When my brief final years are gone
shall learn to turn away
And cram those open eyes with day.

'Margot'
From W. B. Yeats's manuscript

Overleaf:
'Weep not'
Poem by Margot Ruddock amended and rewritten by W. B. Yeats

WEEP NOT.

. . . .

that mask !

Weep not! beloved, for the grey of tears
Is like a liquid veil upon thine eyes.
There is another dawn to suffer sighs,
There is another day for fevered fears.
Weep not! for weeping so thou can'st not see
How little threads of comfort may be drawn
Out of another's heart into thine own,
Nor how my own two hands stretch forth to thee.

And if at Dawn the little threads should break
Weep not again, beloved, for my sake.

. . . .

What matters if another dawn bring sighs
another mortal day its pains & fears
weep not a weeping eye can never see
How great a web of comfort can be drawn
out of another heart into their own
nor even of two hands stretched out to thee
~~at dawn if dawn the web of comfort break~~
when if the Dawn the web of comfort break
Mock at the dawn beloved for my sake

troubles without weakening your capacity for action and yet keep your philosophy you have attained wisdom and character. You have increased my pleasure in my work, for I feel that in working with the Swami on our new translation of the Upanishads I shall henceforth feel what it feels to you. It is far wilder and more profound than the Bhagavad-Gita.

I do not like your recent poems. You do not work at your tecnic (I cannot spell the most familiar words because of my illness – this is my first real letter) you take the easiest course – leave out the rhymes or choose the most hackneyed rhymes, because – damn you – you are lazy. Leave off verse for a time. When your technic is sloppy your matter grows second-hand – there is no difficulty to force you down under the surface – difficulty is our plough. Yours affectionately,

W. B. Yeats

47

            14c Westbourne Gardens

Darling Yeats,

So many thanks for your letter. I am so glad you are really better.

You are very kind about my play. I am afraid too kind. I wrote another that is no good. I cannot write just now even if I wanted to, the will is not mine! I think a bit of theatre may be forthcoming, I have hopes of the man in whose companies I once worked who has regard for my acting, and who now thinks I am a religious maniac! (Through no desire of mine to be thought one.) However maybe that's all an illusion too.

I want to start a Fable. A Man who was never happy and wanted to get out of things, tried to cram everything into one life, and to do this had to give everything that ever came his way, but presently he found that nobody would take what he could give so he became very angry and started to take everything he could lay his hands on, and expected that he would have to come back and back, but when he died he found it was all right because he had given all through taking.

I live in the most strange state of dreaming *all over* so that I am fully and more than ever awake all over. People say I am mad, it doesn't matter, they've always said it from my first husband onwards.

There's a highly technical book by a man called Deussen about the philosophy of the Upanishads.[1] It is a sort of scientific perusal of them rather like a timetable, but I like it because I can supply the non-technical side myself.

I hear the Swami is going to India or maybe. My cat is going to have kittens. I wish we could talk together. Love,

Margot

48

10/4/36

Darling W. B. Y.,

I must write to you about this book which is about 'that God the Atman', it says, 'the knowledge of the Atman depends upon a kind of free grace, only by the man he chooses is he comprehended, to him the Atman reveals his essence, he who perceives the Atman and is conscious that "I am he" what desire what love could he still have for the body racked with pain. He who knows Brahman as truth, knowledge, infinite hidden in

[1] Dr Paul Deussen, *The Philosophy of the Upanishads*, translated from the German by the Rev. A. S. Geden (Edinburgh, Clark, 1906).

the cavity of the heart and in the farthest space he obtains every wish in communion with Brahman the omniscient.'[1]

I write this because it concerns myself, this last bit about the wish is a certain stage I think one does not reach beyond worldly things, and being beyond worldly things may wish for them, and take them like my man in the fable to give them back; I read somewhere else that Mahatma should take worldly things in order that he may give them back in a purer form.

There is another paragraph that I have found to be true with myself.

'By continued meditation his body by a process of gradual refinement becomes composed in turn of earth, water, fire, air, and ether until finally *he thinks only in and* through himself.' I have only just realised this myself.

Recently in tight corners I have said 'God what shall I do?' and there followed a process of thinking and reasoning quite unbeknown in the old days, as though God said I will think for you, in you, so that you will realise I will always think in you, if you ask I am yourself, and after this process of reasoning and thinking sudden conclusion and decision, and once when I had dismissed the whole thing from my mind and was in my bath I suddenly said aloud with my whole being, 'I want such and such a thing' that I had doubted whether I ought to have wanted.

You remember that old servant Jane who died last autumn? She is often here, I feel her presence, she brings great peace. I cannot see her with my naked eye, but in my mind's eye like I saw you when you were ill, I cannot hear her if she speaks, it is not that I have been thinking of her but when I am unhappy she comes.

It is all most wild and most profound and miraculous! And the wilder one is oneself the quicker one finds truth, don't think

[1] These passages are not from Deussen's book but from a translation of the Upanishads which he quotes.

I'm mad will you, I couldn't bear that, if everyone else says I'm mad I don't mind, but not you. Otherwise I shall know I am mad. Love,

Margot

P.S. Will you give my love to Swami if you see him.

49

[Undated, mid-April 1936?]   14c Westbourne Gardens

'He' is but a word.
Spirit 'He' is joy
In all living things
Thine own self is He
Seeking 'Him' in self
Thou shalt come to know
One with Him thou art
Bird and Beast and Bough.

Darling Yeats,

How pleased I was to get a letter from you and hear you are better. Lots and lots of things are happening but they have nothing to do with the stage! Only the stage people! This all very secretly exciting and amusing to watch.

I believe Jo's Bar was called The Hole in the Wall, funny if you'd taken the same villa I was thinking of! I am better now I feel I am a bit of good to somebody. The feeling of being useless is so dreadful – I am also busy drawing coal [?] houses and writing bits of verse occasionally. The theatre man may take a theatre in Manchester once nightly and the more I refuse to go the keener he gets! I think he will end by buying a London theatre for me and plastering my name in searchlights!

If my career on the stage is given me it will be in circumstances in which I am able to accept. The Crewe business had
significance in other ways I find. If it isn't I don't mind as long
as I have work of some sort.

It is awful when one's very work is taken away though. Did
you read that Avadhut Gitre?[1] The Swami gave me one. I like
it the best of all, I long to walk about naked in the wilds of
India.

A friend of mine said, 'You are much too attractive, all the
Mahatmas would come and make love to you. I'm sure it must
be very dull for them.' That's all he knows. All my love,

Margot

50

Monday, 20th/4/36   14c Westbourne Gardens

Darling W. B. Y.,

I suppose because you said I should leave verse alone, I
have written a poem which runs as follows:

> Where passions drain away
> The deep trench of the soul
> Keeps its serenity,
> Secret, unbroken, cool.
>
> Though amorously should
> The flesh to flesh submit
> Though limb unites into limb
> Soul has no will in it.

[1] The Awadhoota Gita, the Swami's translation from Sanskrit.

But as a bird may wing
Her change from mood to mood
The will of God is hers
She is the will of God.

There can be no agony to breed a poem for me now because I really don't mind what I do, and if I am put into an agony in order that I should react in such and such a way I should not consider it fair to write a poem because of the half-realisation all the time (which somehow does not dull one, strangely enough) that agony has a purpose.

I feel you see, as though agony were no longer a personal matter, as though in fact Margot was dead personally, but being kept on as it were and allowed her own peculiarities as before to to serve a purpose (myself primarily, of course, I hope and believe).

I live as it happens because I must (and always liked doing so if you remember!).

The reason I suppose things are hard is as you say, difficulty is a plough. And one's life depends upon how much one can stand. When one gets to be able to stand almost anything I suppose naturally one is made use of, and why things are made so difficult is also I suppose to drive one on out of it. And why they drive one out of it is because they have better prospects to offer elsewhere!

The other day I wrote Ashley Dukes about a book he had of mine and he offered me seats for *Murder in the Cathedral* at the Mercury by Eliot. So I went taking Raymond with me. And *very well* it played too. Very simply done and well acted. The chorus work was particularly good. Miss Fogarty I understand produced *them*.

It's really marvellously written I think. I feared it would seem very orthodox church, but there were bits I had forgotten which made up for all that.

I liked your remark about architecture and the bride's cake, lovely.

Robert Speaight played Becket, he was good in that part although Raymond after the performance reminded me of the three new rules of acting recently proclaimed which run,

1. Not like Robert Speaight
2. Not like Robert Speaight
3. *And* – not like Robert Speaight!

I see he has just published a new book *Angel in the Mist* well reviewed in *Sunday Times* last.

Have had quite a gay week (last), and a new evening frock. Film work hovers round me that I cannot snatch, it is so *infuriating*. I wrote to Swami how infuriating it was to have work offered and then snatched away, and perhaps the reason they snatched it away was to make me write to him *about* its being infuriating. God must have someone to worry about. I'm sure it's very difficult to be man and God at the same time – rather like being a chameleon on a striped rug not knowing which colour to turn.

There seems to be a lot of this letter, do write some to me when you can.

Tabby Willow my cat has *four* kittens in the baby's cot, she did. Love

Margot

Short Story
Two *very* rich fleas retired and bought a dog.[1]

[1] Yeats used this anecdote in the dialogue between the two feuding kings in Scene 1 of *The Herne's Egg*:
> *Aedh.* A story is running round
> Concerning two rich fleas.
> *Congal.* We hop like fleas, but war
> Has taken all our riches.
> *Aedh.* Rich, and rich, so rich that they
> Retired and bought a dog. [*Continued overleaf*].

P.S. Idea for a play.

There was once a man who was so frightened of doing wrong he wouldn't do anything he wanted to do, and the powers had a dreadful time turning and twisting things around, when they wanted him to do anything at all they had to make it dreadful for him.

51

24/4/36   14c Westbourne Gardens

Yeats,

Never say I do not work, for I am sitting from morn till night over a poem so bad so bad so *Bad*. Do you know that you have made poetry, my solace and my joy, a bloody grind I hate!

If we are in our natural state we write like the Swami (in his native). 52 poems of sheer *ecstasy* in a day.

I loathe poetry, I loathe working at it for given grammar and words (of which I have not enough), poetry should *not* be worked at. Scrub floors and sweat in offices but do not sweat at poetry which is spiritual sweat! And to make it physical sweat as well is to condemn it with all other earthly things.

Congal. Finish the tale and say
   What kind of dog they bought.
Aedh. Heaven knows.
Congal.   You must have thought
   What kind of dog they bought.
Aedh. Heaven knows.
Congal.   Unless you say,
   I'll up and fight all day.
Aedh. A fat, square, lazy dog,
   No sort of scratching dog.

James Stephens said, 'There is always poetry when there is not love', now for me not even that!

I know what you will say, one must get the physical as well as spiritual labour – why? To read verse toiled and woven with pen-labour tires one, and that is just what verse should not do. One reads a novel or a play to tire one, verse should refresh. Even descriptive verse. One doesn't want to sit for hours unravelling it like you'll have to this poem of mine (I hope!) when I send it which I dare not yet.

Why should we complicate ourselves so much when *in the end* we have to go back to simplicity, to *nothing* but *Being*. Why? The things I wrote of old may not have technique but they have a dashed sight more exaltation than anything and I think 'Sea Shell' the best poem of the lot *since*.[1]

[Unsigned]

52

27/4/36   14c Westbourne Gardens

Darling Yeats,

I am literally sitting all day at these poems which *start* by being so complicated I have to simplify. I will send some more in a day or so as I shall now sit down and write within the next few months all the poems I shall ever write, and if they are not good it's my fault.

Thanks so much for your letter. There was nothing about Robert Speaight's acting that has not been done in my experience, he was himself, which was good in that part, and his voice is good. He will never be a brilliant actor emotionally, or by sheer beauty of personality, he may be a restrained sensitive

[1] See Appendix A, note on Letter 16, page 120.

actor in certain parts, but he will be no *character* actor. Still it doesn't matter what one is I've decided, it's always the people who have nothing in their favour who make something of themselves. But I will write something to live in this next year or die, even if it's dozens of scraps.

Do you like the rhythms of these?

Margot

I cannot go and talk to people you know unless I meet them, and we did not meet.

Yeats had undertaken to select and to write the introduction to a volume of Margot Ruddock's poems, which eventually appeared under the title of The Lemon Tree (Dent, 1937). *He included seven of her poems in* The Oxford Book of Modern Verse, *which was published on 19 November 1936.*

53

4/5/36   14c Westbourne Gardens

Dear W. B. Y.,

Here are poems for you to select from. I put some early ones in as I thought you might take about two just to get a sequence. 'Birth', 'Sea Shell' perhaps.[1]

Do you think I should call myself Margot Ruddock for them or do you think just 'Margot' or would that sound like a pose? I will ring you later, doesn't matter if you are not there, so don't worry about what time.

Margot

I am going to a music shop to have my tune taken down and

[1] See Appendix A, pages 120, 123.

on my way to solicitor now – shall naturally only show the portion of letter that concerns me.[1]

The growing sense of frustration which is evident in some of the preceding letters, together with domestic worries, caused Margot Ruddock to suffer a nervous breakdown early in May. This led to the events which she describes in subsequent letters as her 'Adventures'. The following account of them was eventually published in The Lemon Tree, *immediately after Yeats's introduction. Yeats's suggested heading for this section was 'The Catastrophe' but the title she chose was 'Almost I Tasted Ecstasy'.*

ALMOST I TASTED ECSTASY

I

I had been a failure at housekeeping. I had to spend money I had set aside for the child's future. Things could only get worse, I had failed to get employment as an actress. It seemed best that I should die but I thought, 'if I am a good poet I have the right to live'. For a week I sat at the typewriter, then I thought 'I will go to Majorca, Yeats will tell me if I am a good poet, Shree Purohit Swami* if I have a right to live'.

I took a second class ticket but at Victoria found that I could go third. I went to the ticket office to change my ticket. There was an old gentleman talking a long time to the clerk, at last I thrust out my ticket but the old gentleman said 'Madam you must learn to wait'. I must have stared at him for he added 'You will know me the next time we meet'. He went away and the clerk asked me for my ticket; I said 'There comes a time when

---

[1] See Appendix C, page 133, for a letter which may have some bearing on this passage.

* He had come to Majorca to work with me at a translation of 'The Upanishads'. W. B. Y.

nothing matters' and went out, I could not give him my ticket.

In the night between Paris and Barcelona I could not sleep but wrote a great deal, I wrote 'Cold Swan', it was cold because it had not the courage to die.

COLD SWAN

Cold swan, die,
I can bear that you should die
That I must hear you singing;
Can be silent;
Not disturb.
Wing out to death cold Swan, out through the cold.

Death brings more than life;
Have we not ached a little and enough
Yet, to our own selves bound,
Fashioned miracles, broken vows, all silence.
Break from the self break miracle,
What if this should be our hour
And we not sing together;
Fashion me afresh;
I am no broken toy, my toys are burnt;
You cannot take my tears;
None may take what is not his own.

In the morning I looked into the sun and prayed that if I had to die it should be in such a state of ecstasy I should not have to cry out or have any pain.

2

At the villa there was a long verandah running completely round, I saw many windows but no door but a voice told me to turn round the corner to the right. I came to an open window and there Mrs Yeats was standing, I told Yeats that if I could not write a poem that would live I must die. He went through my poems but said I must work at each until it was perfect. I said, 'How can I made them perfect? I am too strong to die, too weak to live'. Then I thought that if I died my poems would live in my stead. Later Yeats showed me some book and said 'I cannot understand the punctuation of this', I read the words:

'This was one fulfilment, without the tomb
The other one in life was just as sad'.*

I thought 'there should be a comma after fulfilment', and that it meant I must die. Yeats read some poem about the sea. I slipped out when nobody was looking. I went slowly down to the shore through the rain; I thought 'if I am to die something will help me', I stood on the rocks and could not go into the sea because there was so much in life I loved, then I was so happy at not having to die I danced.

I got a room at a pension where Shree Purohit Swami was staying. He lent me clothes for I was wet through, I had come away without money; I thought 'if I stay here people will think I came to see him before he left for India and not knowing that he is beyond all human interests blame him. I will go and see my friends in Barcelona where my baby was born two years ago'. He lent me money and I left next evening.

3

On the boat I thought 'Perhaps somebody must die if [I] live', I asked God not to let anybody die.

At Barcelona I walked up the Rambla, and I thought, 'All these flowers are mine but not until I have died for them'. I went to see a friend; a dog that belonged to an other friend

* I do not remember these lines; they may be, like much in the passage, part of her dream. W. B. Y.

that knew me jumped up and said 'Your dog, Margot'. We went down the town and sat in a cafe and talked of Indian thought and sex symbolism in Indian Mythology, I was disturbed, I do not know why, I felt a violent nervous shock. After lunch I left my friend, I took my handbag and hurried down to the sea, I wanted to get out of doors and think. Before leaving something inside me said 'It will be very cold tonight'. I thought of my poem:

> At first I thought that I would see
> How very cold the moon could be
> And then I knew that I could learn
> The icy coldness of the moon.

I lay on the grass by the boats and repeated what I had said on the boat about nobody dying for me, then I closed my eyes and thought I would sleep.

Suddenly the sun got very hot, there were shots in the sky; I opened my eyes, my bag was gone. Then I thought 'Swami has died instead of me'. I had my writing pad and I wrote 'I wander an outcast. I cannot live or die'. I got up and walked back to the town, men by the shore jeered at me; many eyes followed me, I was suddenly filled with strong sexual passion. Horrified I thought 'I must control myself'. In a few minutes I had recovered. I sat on a seat and wondered who had died. I thought 'I must go back to Palma and find out'. While I was sitting on the seat I heard 'Make yourself a prostitute for me as I did for you'. I tried to find my way home but could not. I thought 'if I could find the British Consul he would help'. I wandered for hours and then asked a Guardia to bring me to the Consul, we walked from one place to another, I was so hungry that I told the Guardia but said I had no money. He brought me to a cafe and a man offered me food, I was hungry and as I looked down at the coffee and roll it said to me 'This is my body and blood which was shed for you'. I thanked the man who smiled and went away and I ate the food. Presently, because we could not find the Consul, the Guardia took me to a Pension, but the woman looked at me doubtfully and said she had no room. I said 'I am a prostitute, and outcast from all Nations, I wander without hope of death', she said 'No, no, you are tired, there is a room here'. She gave me food but I could not eat; it seemed like eating myself; I thought 'All Nature will die if I eat', but in the morning I was hungry, I said 'God can I have some food please', a man came through the door with coffee and rolls and said, 'For you, Senora', I ate and wrote my thanks in French and English, and the Proprietor took me back to my friends who did not know what had happened to me.

That afternoon we went for a walk in some gardens with the dog, there were masses of flowers and we sat and talked. I kept on talking for I felt such a bliss creeping over me I could not endure it and wanted to get back to myself.

It was a physical bliss as though I were dissolved to joy but it worried me because I couldn't explain to my friend about it, and my mind went on thinking and worrying. I played with the dog as I had used to do and suddenly it said: 'Run, run for your life', it did not speak with a voice but I heard it in my mind, I thought it meant the bliss was dangerous and I must run to shake it off. I hurried to my friend's home and when at the door asked if I might take the dog for a run as it was very important. She stared at me. We ran and the dog said 'What shall I be in my next life? Do something now which I cannot do and that will decide'. I jumped on the back of a van horse. The dog, arching its neck proudly, said 'I shall be a horse'. I jumped down and we ran away.

4

It was towards morning, I had slept little, my friends were anxious. I felt myself floating out in an ecstasy but didn't dare

95

let myself go, I thought I should die if I did. I got up and walked about the flat, I asked a young man for a cigarette, we sat talking, I felt great despair – dawn came very slowly, I thought 'the dawn cannot come because I did not go into the ecstasy and die'. We had breakfast, my friends thought me insane. I went to the front door to try and get out, I thought 'if I can get back to Majorca Yeats will know I'm not insane', my friends locked the door, I fought them, the young man tried to put me in a room I did not like because something said it was not the right room. I fought him although I knew he was a friend, and fought with them all when they tried to put me in that room. They put me in another room which seemed friendly, the walls and the woodwork almost part of myself. I began to sing, making up words and music, something about God being everywhere and in everything. I remembered I had the Swami's slippers. He had lent them to me when I got wet in Majorca, I wore them coming to Barcelona but had taken them off, they were in the other room. I thought 'I must return them, I must go to Majorca'. I stopped singing, hammered on the door and called to my friends. They did not hear for they were talking to the Guardia who had come to take me to an asylum,* quickly I ran to the window, knew I must escape somehow. I got out of the window, the walls were of rough sandstone, and the windows underneath had ironwork of some kind. I climbed down some way, I had no shoes on which helped, at last I saw a gray roof below. If I could reach that I could jump from there to the ground. I dropped on to it and went through the roof and seemed to fall a long way. After the first pain there was no pain, I had fallen into a Barber's shop and people rushed to pick me up but I walked out; outside were the Guardia on their horses. I was pleased at having defeated them and talked to the horses. They took me to a Clinic. I fought them but they tied me down and put me to sleep. When I woke I had a

* No; to an hospital. W. B. Y.

burning thirst. I asked for water. They wheeled me to be X-rayed and I sang some poems, the men who wheeled me and one of the Sisters sang Spanish songs, the men danced and clapped their hands, then another Sister came and hushed us up.

I could not sleep, my leg hurt, a woman groaned in the next bed, and there was a man who had had a street accident on his way to the Palma boat. I thought I had done that too by not dying.

In the morning I was better, somebody had sent roses and I had their scent all day. The Sisters asked me to sing at their shrine and I sang a poem there, they let me walk through the ward and asked me to sing; all the men were terribly injured, I still thought I had done it by not dying. They brought me to the women's ward, the women too were terribly injured. Nobody seemed to notice me there.

I walked down the stairs and out into the sun. They had given me a man's nightshirt, and I had on my coat and skirt, but no shoes and stockings, my leg was in plaster.

I went to the house where my friend lived to get the slippers to take to Majorca, but the house seemed shut up. I walked slowly to the boat. It was a long way but I felt no pain. I was at peace and smelled flowers all the way. I felt hungry but had no money. I thought 'I will sell my rings to buy my passage', but I had no passport. I crept into the hold of the boat, a cat came up and looked at me, I started to sing softly, I remember I sang:

> Sea-starved, hungry sea,
> In a stretched hand humility,
> Lapped there in a dream stand
> Shut eyes to the sea sand
> Knowing that the sea is there
> Drink deep . . . O weeping cry . . .
> O my love leaned a little from me.

After, I thought, 'This boat is mine, I have always wanted

a boat and this is it'. Some sailors came, I offered them my rings if they would take me to Palma. They talked a lot and were kind but said I must go with them to the Police Station.

MARGOT RUDDOCK

Yeats's introduction to The Lemon Tree *and his letters of 22 May 1936 to Olivia Shakespear and to Dorothy Wellesley help to fill in some details. Apparently Margot Ruddock arrived at Casa Pastor early one morning towards the middle of May and wandered away while Yeats was reading through some of the many poems she had sent him and which, for the most part, he had left unread. The Yeatses next saw her, a few days later, as a result of an appeal from the British Consul at Barcelona, where they found her sitting up in bed at the Enfermeria Evangelica, writing her account of these events. Her sanity seemed fully recovered, and they arranged for her return to England in charge of a nurse. Yeats wrote to Shri Purohit Swami on 25 May giving a brief account of the events in Barcelona and mentioning that she had written 'A strange account of her madness which I shall publish with a selection from her poems'. As subsequent letters show, he soon had second thoughts about this, for a time. The Yeats papers include a draft of her account ('The Catastrophe') in his own handwriting. It differs slightly from her published account in that his draft mentions her husband, Raymond Lovell, by name and there are a few other minor changes. As Hone mentions in his biography of Yeats, paragraphs on the episode had appeared in the London papers, 'and oral traditions were numerous and contradictory. Both Yeats and the Swami . . . received anonymous letters' so one can understand the guarded terms of Yeats's introduction to* The Lemon Tree *which he wrote partly in June, partly in December 1936.*

54

14c Westbourne Gardens

Dearest W. B. Y.,

We arrived home quite safely in spite of the fact that Matron frequently lost or rather mislaid tickets and I teased her saying she'd never be the same again after knowing me!

I gave her a poem for her husband to sing. He is I believe a Russian. She was most kind.

Will you let me know what money you spent on wines for me, or your wife spent and I will give it to you, or send it. The newspapers have not been, but Raymond showed me the cuttings which I don't think will do any harm to any of us. I do hope not, just to say I had gone with my poems to you, and then in Barcelona fallen from a balcony and had concussion. What a blessing I did climb from the window, I believe they would have shut me up had I not done so.

Did I tell you about the cat on the ship? That would finish the adventures rather well perhaps.

I thought *Cold Swan and Other Poems* would be a good title. If not *The Lemon Tree*. The press have just rung and asked if they could take photographs. I said I really didn't want any publicity, but if they liked they could say that everyone had been very kind especially the B. Consul in Spain.

There have been quite enough photographs of me in the papers!

Mrs Foden sent flowers.[1] I thanked her through Raymond over the phone and told her I thought I was going to stay with my brother immediately. My love to you,

Margot

[1] Mrs Foden had been active in helping the Institute of Indian Mysticism in London in 1934. She was a friend of the Swami and had returned from a visit to Majorca in February 1936.

Yeats and his wife sailed for England shortly after Margot Ruddock had returned there. He wrote from Casa Pastor on 22 May 1936 to Dorothy Wellesley, accepting her invitation to stay with her: 'After this wild week—not without its fineness—' he wrote, 'I long for your intellect and sanity. Hitherto I have never found these anywhere but at Coole.' In a postcript he adds, 'My spelling and writing are worse than usual – fatigue, results of Barcelona!' He enclosed a photograph of himself and the Swami. The Swami originally had intended to return to England but in April 1936 news of the illness of his Master, Bhagwan Shri Hamsa, made him decide to return to India. 'He says there are only three people he regrets not seeing again', wrote Yeats to Olivia Shakespear on 26 April 1936: 'Mrs Shakespear, Omar, and Margot Collis'. This wish to see Margot again was of course granted in the most unexpected way by her arrival in Majorca, but his boat sailed shortly after on 13 May.

55

31/5/36   14c Westbourne Gardens

Dear W. B. Y.,

Many thanks for your letter. I do not know if you received mine which the Matron told me to address c/o Mr Short, Palma. She had an idea you were moving I think to some hotel before you left the island.

I would like to see you so much. I wonder if you would care to come here, we could be quiet I think and undisturbed. Or if you prefer I could meet you anywhere as I am quite re-covered but for the limp and several bandages in strange situations on the body!

O what a time I have had, the aunts sent me pamphlets of

'The Oxford Group' (an association that I am told makes a lot of money out of religion), and they said they hoped I would read them, and what a difference God made to one's life, they had seen young girls like me get up radiant and speak at meetings and change their lives completely! (I dread to think what they think I have been doing!)

Raymond thought I had gone to India to an Ashran or Ashpran or something. I said what's that, and he said, some of the monasteries there are nothing but white slave traffic. He wrote to the police in Bombay enquiring about things, and asking what was known of certain people, and saying I had gone out there and if anything evil was known would they stop me on landing.

He had had no reply so they just think him a lunatic, I expect, but I am most anxious to go through my adventures again with you and make quite sure nobody's name suffers through their publication.

Raymond got it into his head that anything not Church of England was what he called inverted Yoga, he as been studying black magic or something. I told him not to dare to talk about such things to me, or to say such things about my friends because I would not stand it, but I am wondering if the Barcelona adventures had anything to do with his aunts who placed cross against crescent according to Raymond, whatever that means, perhaps that's why I was afraid someone had died.

I am now waiting to let this flat before going into one small room. My child sleeps with Molly my Irish maid for whom I thank God, as the aunts said they could not have her even for a few weeks and I see her in the day. Raymond doesn't want to keep her for me as far as I can make out. He has done several very kind things though. I will keep her and pay something to Molly for her to sleep there. This flat is the problem.

I wonder if you would ring me on Tuesday, as I do not know what time you arrive.

Maybe it would be better if we met in town as you may be tired. This No. is *Bay 5091*, they have cut the phone off but people can still ring us I hope till Tuesday. Yours with love,

Margot

I would like to get something in about that first written blessing and the suffusion of joy it brought. That might shut up the aunts.

That Yeats had decided not to see Margot Ruddock on his return is clear from his earlier letter to Olivia Shakespear written on 22 May 1936, while he was still at Casa Pastor. 'I accepted financial responsibility and she was despatched to England and now I won't be able to afford new clothes for a year,' he wrote. 'When her husband wrote it had not been to send money, but to congratulate her on the magnificent publicity. The paragraph you saw is certainly his work. Will she stay sane? It is impossible to know.

'When I am in London I shall probably hide because the husband may send me journalists and because I want to keep at a distance from a tragedy where I can be no further help. I am going to Lady Gerald Wellesley's and shall go as soon as possible.' He arrived in London about 2 June, and, after spending a few days 'in obscurity' at the Savile Club, went to Penns in the Rocks, probably about 7 June 1936. The poet mentioned in Letter 56 must have been Dorothy Wellesley, but I cannot find any clue as to the identity of the critic. During his visit Yeats was preparing an introduction to a selection of Margot Ruddock's poems for the July number of the London Mercury, *of which R. A. Scott-James was the editor.*

56

Penns in the Rocks, Withyham, Sussex
Wednesday (I think) [c. 9 June 1936]

My dear Margot,

I read out those fragments of your 'Snatchings',[1] etc. to two people here, one a fine poet, one an even finer critic, though no poet. At first a little hostile they were conquered – 'You are right – they are all you say, but what suffering!' I asked both to read through your account of the Barcelona escapade, both were vehement for its postponement for the present. Published now it would get us both into great trouble. You would be accused of publishing it for 'publicity' reasons and I of allowing you in your first moment of excitement to publish what might compromise your future. I have therefore asked Scott-James to allow me to substitute an essay on your work with selections of your poems. Both your critics here have urged me to greatly enlarge my extracts from your work in the anthology. I do not yet know if this is possible. I will write later. I am suffering from too much work and too little sleep so must rest. Yours,

W. B. Yeats

57

10/6/36   14c Westbourne Gardens

My dear W. B. Y.

Many thanks for your letter. If you really think the Adventures must not come out *by themselves* – but I cannot see why

[1] See Appendix A, pages 124–7.

when a thing is true one should be afraid. In any case there will be those who say this, that and the other, if there were not no one would be interested – we must set fire to be able to quench it, otherwise there is no interest, I do not want so much interest in *me*, I want interest in these *Adventures*, I feel they are most important and I do want them in the book even if they do not appear now. They are *my poem*, all the other but leads up to it. I must get them done somehow, I don't want the book without them, all the other is just personal point of view. Those adventures are not, they are the beginning of my life, and if I go to India in the later years and write of that, they will be remembered, and people will follow.

I said to you it would put me right with my friends, it is *more* than that, I have never minded much what people thought (except to shut me up!). Look upon me as a Nancy Price with a mission to fulfil if you like![1] After all one's got to have a mission – I don't want to have to break another knee to get to spiritual things; it's most painful afterwards, don't let it be wasted, as long as it comes out in the book as the introduction with a lovely photograph of me cleverly hidden at the end of the book so as not to look obvious I think it will interest people, and that's what I've got to do, not just write verse and act and do what everyone's been doing for centuries.

I said, 'It's time someone threw away
        The old shag and the new
        And both pipes.'

Let them say what they like, if we don't do anything common we are not charged with it. I beg you not to go too much into committee regarding vital issues. It is what all the politicians have done for centuries and the result is they never get anywhere. It does not matter *what* one does it is the *reason* one

[1] i.e. Nancy Price's dedication to the People's National Theatre movement.

does it. Do not tire yourself too much – would it help if I went to see Scott-James and talked it over with him at your suggestion? Your Love,

Margot

58

My Dear Margot,

I enclose Scott-James's letter.[1] I have sent him 'A Note on Margot Ruddock' with seven of her lyrics. The note contains many extracts from 'Snatchings' etc.

Let me conduct your 'publicity' for a little.

I grow more and more admiring of your genius and so will others. You have an intensity no writer of this time can show in the expression of spiritual suffering.

I was in my bath when you phoned having spent the whole morning on your work. Yours,

W. B. Yeats

[1] The Ruddock papers include a letter from the editor of the *London Mercury*, R. A. Scott-James, dated 9 June 1936, to Margot Ruddock. It states that he has not yet received the promised selection of her poems from Yeats and adds: 'I have a letter from him this morning in which he says that he thinks we should not publish the statement in the form in which he first presented it to me.'

59

11/6/36   14c Westbourne Gardens

My Dear W. B. Y.,

Thanks so much for your letter this morning enclosing Scott-James's. Perhaps it is as well the Adventures should come later then.[1] Thank you very much for sending the poems.

Mrs Foden explains through her solicitors that she gave me five pounds, and apologises for interference. I think it has frightened her, most certainly she did not give me five pounds. Raymond says she did not give it to him though offered money. If I thought she had given him money I would pay it back but how am I to know!!

As I do not want weeks of correspondence, I am instructing my solicitors to write letting the matter drop, and offering to return the five pounds if she can prove she gave it and saying there is no ill feeling as long as she minds her own business.

I want to get the technique of simple blank verse right. Here is a song I have written music for but haven't had it taken down yet.

> Naked against thy breast I lie
> Against thy warm heart press naked
> To drink thy mercy
> Earth, one with thee not perishable.
> Sweet it is to drink thy sweetness,
> Sweet to drain my tears to thy dark bosom
> Tears that are drawn
> From out thy silences,
> Love leaps miracled from thy stern disciplines
> Thou only art first of laws,

[1] i.e. in *The Lemon Tree*.

Thy never failing law the Spring
Returns itself to thee as offering
The flowers keep thine austerity
Once flowering and twice flowering
The oaks age and the evergreen
All with mixed sighs obey to thee
O One, proven Deity in all things living
I who obey thee am thine
Thou, my bread, life, wine.

I have a good chance of letting my flat, shall know by the end
of the week about it. No news from my theatrical manager. I
told him not to bother to answer unless he had a vacancy – I
have a horror in my mind of monasteries. I cannot imagine why
the Swami thought I should ever wish to go to India to be shut
in a monastery. In a cave yes, but not *indoors*. The idea of being
shut in is so terrible, is that what they do if one goes there, do
you think? I thought one was allowed to make pilgrimages and
sleep in woods. What could he have meant when he told you I
was not ready for the monastery yet? Do tell me what you
think, it worries me so much. The Swami was not shut in a
monastery, was he? Love,

Margot

*Yeats had enlisted the help of W. J. Turner in preparing the music
for the Cuala Broadsides to which Dorothy Wellesley contributed
several ballads, for Turner was a musical critic as well as a poet.
Yeats wrote to Dorothy Wellesley on 25 June 1936 that one of
Turner's poems 'rends my heart':*

> *But when a man is old, married and in despair*
> *Has slept with the bodies of many women;*
> *Then if he meets a woman whose loveliness*
> *Is young and yet troubled with power . . .*
> *Terrible is the agony of an old man*

The agony of incommunicable power
Holding its potency that is like a rocket
That is full of stars.

60

June 14 [1936]   Penns in the Rocks

My dear Margot,

When Turner's foreign lady is taking down your music, do not forget the settings to Lady Dorothy's two love ballads. She is longing for them. If you promise them in your 'bread and butter letter', she will be pleased.[1] Yours,

W. B. Yeats

61

15/6/36   14c Westbourne Gardens

Dear W. B. Y.,

Here is the statement,[2] I have retyped it as several things I had told you were very inaccurate and on page four about the 'bliss' was too long to write in.

In the first place I have left out 'The Swami will tell me me whether I may live'. I certainly never thought that, and shouldn't have asked him! Then the phrase, 'How can I give

---

[1] This must imply something other than a visit to Penns in the Rocks at that time. Perhaps Dorothy Wellesley was paying Margot Ruddock for the settings.

[2] i.e. her Adventures, revised for inclusion in *The Lemon Tree*. Not all the revisions mentioned here were carried out in the published text.

perfection, I am too weak to live too strong to die.' That I never said to you in Majorca, what I said to you was 'I cannot give perfection therefore I can't take it.' All my life the theatre in me, the slightest exaggeration of fact, has made me a liar!

My mother thought I told lies because once in a farmhouse I saw the farmer give his dog an enormous bone of mutton with much meat on it, and came back and told her he had given his dog a whole leg of mutton.

I must have thought that a good phrase to put in when I told you I said that.

I have left out mention of dying until after 'Cold Swan' in the train. Actually that was when it came upon me very strongly. When I left here I had very shadowy thoughts about it not formed at all. The inset on page 3 is true not just put in.

The bit about the boat being mine on page 7 I have thought since but put in because I thought it might have lyrical value. I left out about the cherries, forgot them, do you think them important?[1]

I send you a poem 'Burnish' meaning clean off Rust – Sweep on Doom where the phlegm phrase comes, three scraps.[2]

I'd like 'Burnish' in if possible because I want to say that 'Becoming' does not make one *less* individual.

Love and hope you're well.

Margot

---

[1] In the draft in Yeats's hand occur the words 'I found the friend who had talked about India. She gave me cherries and the cherries said "Take my life." '

[2] See Appendix A, page 127.

62

14c Westbourne Gardens

Dear W. B. Y.,

The songs are taken down and are being copied from the rough by Mr Turner and an awfully nice Polish girl who is rather beautiful I think.

Three of Lady Wellesley's – I took one from her book and four of yours.

> 'Holy Land of Ireland'
> 'Penny Brown Penny'
> 'Do not love too long'
> 'Old men admiring themselves'.

I think they will be quite good. We varied the keys. 'Holy Land of Ireland' quite low so it can be sung by man or woman.

Do you think I should leave myself '*Collis*' in the Anthology? Or should I see whether it is possible to change that before it is too late?[1]

Here is the 'Everlasting Night' poem, and others – will finish tomorrow as it is dark and I want to go to bed and read by candlelight it increases my enjoyment of reading. Why?

Wednesday [June 17]

I do not know if you already have 'Down Stream' and 'Reedy Marsh' nor what scraps you selected. I want the Atman one in if possible, even if it's not intellectual, can it go in? There are several versions, this is the simplest. Did you mean you had ten poems only with the Anthology ones?[2] Surely there must

---

[1] She appears as Margot Ruddock in *The Oxford Book of Modern Verse*.

[2] *The Lemon Tree* includes twenty-one of her poems, including the seven which appeared in *The Oxford Book of Modern Verse*.

be more, or perhaps better not to put Anthology ones in the book.

I have no time to type these as you said you might leave tomorrow. Will you let me know if these are all right? Don't alter the meaning of the Atman one. Best love,

Margot

The London Mercury *of July 1936 included 'Poems: by Margot Ruddock with Prefatory Notes on the Author by W. B. Yeats'.*

63

28/6/36   14c Westbourne Gardens

Dear W. B. Y.,

I want to thank you so much for all you've done for me.

My husband *did* take a cheque for £5 from Mrs Foden. She produced it! I sent it to her immediately through my solicitors.

On Wednesday I go to my brother's, my address will be

> Six Larches,
> Hartfield,
> Sussex.

I hope you did not suffer from your journey. I have been drawing the ships by Battersea Bridge in pastel chalks on brown sugar paper. I enjoy it and it feeds my feverish craving for the sea in some peculiar way.

Also I have been drawing flowers which please me so much that when I get my room I shall colour wash the walls a light colour and paint a dado of flowers, or draw them with chalks and varnish over the top to stop smudging.

No other news, I am busy with a poem which I will send

when it is finished as much as I can finish it. I like 'Attracta' very much in your play[1] because one could make her anything one chose, either a rather timid secretive woman unaware of her own voluptuousness, or else a cold, blade-cold woman with no actual voluptuousness but fierceness – or else one might play her completely oneself, and let them guess *which* one really was.

I would wear drapy clothes for her that might be worn in a wood or in a drawing-room and if I had beautiful feet no shoes. As I have *not* beautiful feet, sandals, silver sandals perhaps and a silver ribbon round my head!

Always I used to infuriate a certain producer by deciding exactly the clothes I would wear for a certain part before anything.

Never could I think until I knew what I would wear. And then, out of the clothes and me combined came character, mannerisms, etc., for the part. Best love to you,

Margot

The next letter is undated and incomplete. The address indicates that it was written after 28 June 1936, when she was still at Westbourne Gardens: Yeats's letter to the Swami from Palma (25 May 1936) had stated that before she left Barcelona 'she wrote to her brother that her financial relations with her husband must be settled with a solicitor or she would leave him'.

The disturbed nature of this letter may account for her reassurance in the first paragraph of Letter 65.

[1] *The Herne's Egg*, which Yeats must have sent her in manuscript, since it was not published until 1938.

64

My dear W. B. Y.,

I ask you very sincerely and very earnestly to write to the Shri Bhagwan Hamsa's Master at the Ashram, in Sakon district to give him money to come home to Ireland or England and help us to deny in the press in England and India the recent letter sent to Raymond by the police in Bombay in reply to his asking them if anything bad were known about the Ashram.

Raymond showed me their letter which stated that reports were circulating and more enquiries would be made.

The Shri Purohit Swami is my God and his good name and the good name of India are my responsibilities; I beg you as my friend to send for him to safety to this country to do our work together

65

30/7/36   205 Ladbroke Grove

Dear W. B. Y.,

I am busy writing verse and polishing it. I am here ensconced in my room with Tiny, I am afraid my last letter may have worried you a little, please don't let it, I am quite all right. How are the Upanishads going, are they to be published? I do hope so.

Sometimes I find concentration difficult on verse. It is rather difficult wheeling a baby and *not* thinking of something definite, the mind wanders and one gets depressed. I wonder when you will be over, not this winter I suppose. I am very happy really. I always ask too much of life instead of being thankful for all the things around me. I wish you could see my room, it is *enormous* and a big kitchen and all for 14*s* per week. I was very lucky to find it. My sister-in-law and my brother have been most kind. My sister-in-law asked me if I would like to go there during the time they go for their holidays and take Tiny. Have you heard any more about the 'Broadsides' and anything about your new play going on with Ashley Dukes? Write me about the Irish country and flowers. I find flowers bring me peace, flowers, and the talk of a sweet-natured woman I know.

My dearest friend, I cannot ever say how grateful I am to God for giving me your help.

Margot

The next letter is undated, but from its address it must have been written after 30 July 1937. Yeats appeared in four broadcasts in 1937, and in three of them, on 22 April, 3 July and 29 October, Margot Ruddock had taken part. Only in the last of these did Yeats read his own poems as well as the commentary. She sang two of the poems. This seems to be the broadcast referred to here.

66

19b Ladbroke Gardens, W. 11.

[late October – early November 1937]

Dear W. B. Y.,

Someone heard the last broadcast and has given me a song to do for recording.

I sit before my fire or rather the fire God has given me in spite of all my awful mistakes, and have two cats and a dog.

The dog I washed this morning, and it takes her a little time to get used to being without her dogginess. In her next life perhaps she will be a child, she couldn't be more loving anyway, or more faithful through good and bad, and in spite of my impatience with her often. I'm sure it doesn't matter what one is as long as one is harmless. But alas they eat most of the harmless beasts.

I was impressed when last I saw you by the goodness flowing out of you at a moment, then we have to shut it off in this battling world. I am convinced that our food in this country is dreadfully wrong.

The woman upstairs is Irish and she enjoyed your reading so much.

It is a *terrible delight* to go on once one's lamp is lit, but what alas can satisfy us now *but* to go on labouring. I may be a Pavement Artist soon, I hear it is a very paying game, and a friend is coming to see me tomorrow to go into partnership perhaps, but that doesn't mean I'm hard up.

Nobody is allowed to live innocently I think in this country. The young girls have a weight of woe upon them, and happiness doesn't flow from one to the other. So is the child's heritage of peace clutched and grabbed, poor little things. I see them white-faced and worried-looking coming from school they look old at seven! Yours always,

Margot

CONCLUSION

That crazed girl improvising her music,
Her poetry, dancing upon the shore,
Her soul in division from itself
Climbing, falling she knew not where,
Hiding amid the cargo of a steamship,
Her knee-cap broken, that girl I declare
A beautiful lofty thing . . .

Yeats had prefixed this poem to *The Lemon Tree*. In his *Last Poems* it is entitled 'A Crazed Girl' and follows immediately after the poem 'Beautiful Lofty Things', thus linking Margot Ruddock's image with those of O'Leary, John B. Yeats, Standish O'Grady, Augusta Gregory and Maud Gonne, all remembered for some high heroic quality. Perhaps there is some unconscious irony in that it is followed by his poem 'To Dorothy Wellesley', with whom his friendship appears to have become more intimate immediately after his return from Majorca. Curiously no mention of Margot Ruddock is made in Dorothy Wellesley's *Letters on Poetry*. When on 8 June 1937 Yeats sent her a draft of 'Sweet Dancer' it merely elicited the reply, 'No I do not care for your poem "Sweet Dancer".'

Yeats continued to correspond with the Swami until shortly before his own death in 1939. On these particular letters see Appendix C, page 134; excerpts from some of them were published in *The Later Phase of the Development of W. B. Yeats* by S. Mokashi-Punekar (Karnatak University, Dharwar, 1966) but, apart from a brief description of the Barcelona episode dated 25

May 1936, there is no mention of Margot Ruddock. The Swami and his Master, Shri Hamsa, made strenuous efforts to persuade Yeats to lecture in India, but in March 1937 he declined on somewhat unusual grounds. 'Please tell him [Shri Hamsa],' he wrote, 'of the operation I went through in London and say that though it revived my creative power it revived also sexual desire; and that in all likelihood will last me until I die. I believe that if I repressed this for any long period I would break down under the strain as did the great Ruskin.'

The following May he still had vague hopes of going to India, because the final version of *A Vision* was due to appear soon 'and only in India can I find anybody who can throw light upon certain of its problems'. He wrote in July of the same year to condole with the Swami on the death of his Master. After this event, according to Mokashi-Punekar, Shri Purohit Swami became estranged from the Ashram at Lawasha, lectured in various universities and died in hospital after an operation, survived by his widow and two daughters.

Meanwhile, for over a year after the Barcelona episode, Margot Ruddock seemed to have recovered almost completely from her nervous breakdown. She worked with Yeats in three of his 1937 broadcasts reading and occasionally singing his poems, sometimes to her own music. In the broadcast of 3 July, 'He and She' was 'sung by Olive Groves to a setting by Edmund Dulac'. Neither Yeats nor his wife approved of this change, and he wrote to Dulac: 'George's dislike of the singer surprised me even more than her approval of Margot'. In his biography of Yeats, Joseph Hone quotes some relevant recollections by George Barnes, the B.B.C. producer. Barnes thought that Margot had one decided limitation: while she could grasp Yeats's points intuitively during rehearsals, she could not always reproduce the same excellence at actual performances. But she was Yeats's 'chosen instrument' and he recalled her great merits with enthusiasm: 'She possessed one quality which he [Yeats] valued beyond price – the ability to pass naturally from speech to song.' She excelled also in refrains:

> I remember the lilting way in which Yeats taught her to speak
> *Ah, dancer; ah, sweet dancer*[1]
> ... My most vivid memory, however is her use of the lower register of her lovely contralto voice to speak the climax of 'Into the Twilight':
> And God stands winding His lonely horn,
> And time and the world are ever in flight
> And love is less kind than the grey twilight,
> And hope is less dear than the dew of the morn.[2]

Yeats's last broadcast was transmitted on 29 October 1937, but no records survive to show whether or when it was recorded. After the programme had been completed Yeats took Barnes and Margot Ruddock to supper. Hone describes it thus: 'The Ivy was suggested, but it was shut; whereupon Yeats without hesitation, ordered the cabmen to drive to a small "Italian" restaurant, telling on the way of succulent meals he had had there in the past. Alas for his memory, a stern Scottish waitress denied the party drink and the feast consisted of white coffee and hard-boiled eggs.'

This may have been their last meeting: before the end of the year she had a relapse from which she never recovered and was committed to a mental institution. She remained in some lonely twilight of the mind until 1951, when she died at Epsom. She was only forty-four.

Perhaps her real epitaph is that poem in which Yeats, although he changes the setting of her solitary dance by the sea, combines

---

[1] The first poem in the broadcast of 22 April.
[2] In the last broadcast.

those elements of tragedy, pity and terror, with admiration and
regret:

> The girl goes dancing there
> On the leaf-sown, new-mown, smooth
> Grass plot of the garden;
> Escaped from bitter youth,
> Escaped out of her crowd,
> Or out of her black cloud.
> *Ah, dancer, ah, sweet dancer!*
>
> If men come from the house
> To lead her away, do not say
> That she is happy, being crazy;
> Lead them gently astray;
> Let her finish her dance,
> Let her finish her dance.
> *Ah, dancer, ah, sweet dancer!*

APPENDIX A

Letter 7. 'O find me that intricate coverlet': no other text of
this poem has been traced.

Letter 9. 'Split and splayed apart' refers to a typescript poem:

MAN

So that you can play a part
Quarrel with your mistress
And then suckle from your wife
Taking all that she is,

While her body's split and splayed
Birth its own revenge shall sigh
Be on you my blasphemy.

Letter 16. 'O Holy Water' is no. 360 in *O.B.M.V.* Her typescript originally contained a fourth stanza:

O lovely flower
Of belief
I watch thee blossom
Out of grief.

'Sea Shell' was eventually included in *The Lemon Tree:*

SEA SHELL

I saw a shell,
Empty, down in the sand;
It sang 'O Sea
Fasten me to the land'.

It cried 'O Sun
Burn me brittle and gay,
Till my saltness
Has been bitten away'.

I stooped to take him,
Lonely shell, in my hand,
Half scared to break him
Tucked so deep in the sand.

When came a whisper
From the sand up to me
'Soak me with salt
Throw me back in the sea'.

'I take thee, Life' is no. 359 in *O.B.M.V.*
'Child for these undying dreams' apparently refers to a ten-
lined poem of poor quality beginning

Child Life, our undying dreams beget thee, we labour
To bring thee from the womb of Time, the Sepulchre. . .

I can find no poem entitled 'Sea Urchin', but this may have
been the original title of 'As Sand to Sea' in *The Lemon Tree*:

AS SAND TO SEA

1

Pale shimmers
Sand in the bay;
Into the water
It slips away,

2

Breakers gather,
The waters ride,
But the sand
Rests in the tide.

3

So would I,
I could creep
Out of striving
Into sleep,

4

Then might
My spirit run
With a begging bowl
To oblivion.

Letter 19. 'O milk of peace': no other text of this poem has been traced.

Letter 23. 'Thought's a/Poison shoot': this poem appeared under the title 'Poison Shoot' in *The Lemon Tree*.

'The Soul's Cessation' is entitled 'Nirvana' in another type-script draft. It was published with some slight alterations in *The Lemon Tree*, under the title 'Cessation'.

Letter 24. No verses containing the lines quoted appear to have survived.

Letter 27. 'Love Song', with the fourth stanza of this version omitted, is no. 361 in *O.B.M.V.* The fifth and sixth stanzas of 'Autumn, Crystal Eye' are no. 362 in *O.B.M.V.*

Letter 28. These three short poems remained unpublished.

Letter 30. 'Quiet' was published under the title 'And to Quiet' in *The Lemon Tree:*

AND TO QUIET

And to quiet
I shall come,
To the edge
Of my dream.

Enter there
To take my fill
Of all that
Is beautiful,

There shall the
Cold Harlot Night
Mix me into
Her delight.

'Process' was published under the same title in *The Lemon Tree*:

PROCESS

In the gutter
Of the mind
Grief gathers
To gush forth blind.

From the shrill crowd
In the heart
Love stands patiently
Apart.

Letters 42, 49. These two short poems were not published.
Letter 50. 'Where passions drain away'. This poem, with the first line changed to 'Where passion drains away', was published under the title 'Power' in *The Lemon Tree*.
Letter 53. 'Birth' was not published but exists in typescript:

BIRTH

In cold white radiance the lilies lie
Close to my bed, like waxen figures sleeping,
And half my soul forsakes me with a sigh,
Leaving my lonely stricken body weeping
To give to that young life within my own
Burdens of joy and fear and wistfulness,

And wait the blossoming of a flower sown
By beauty in dark pools of tenderness.
Though through the long night hours
Swift burning shall consume me like a fire,
The patience of those flowers
Whispers to me 'Endure!'
And that pain shall not be
So fierce that bitterness corrupts the mind;
After the long red hours of agony
And loneliness and tears broken and blind
Dawn like a cool white hand shall cover me.

'Sea Shell': see note to Letter 16.

Letter 56. 'Snatchings' alludes to ten small typewritten pages which Margot Ruddock sent to Yeats, probably towards the end of April 1936, for their disjointed nature, almost surrealistic in effect, indicates increasing nervous strain. Yeats did not read them until her sudden appearance at the Casa Pastor in early May. A month later, in his introduction to *The Lemon Tree* he describes his immediate reaction:

I sat down with boredom but was soon amazed at my own blindness and laziness. Here in broken sentences, in ejaculations, in fragments of all kinds was a power of expression of spiritual suffering unique in her generation. 'O Song, song harshened, I have leashed you to harshness.' . . . 'I will shut out all but myself and grind, grind myself down to the bone.' . . . 'Follow, follow lest that which you love vanishes. Let it go, let it go' . . . 'Shape me to Eternal Damnation to rid me of the phlegm that spits itself from unbearable cold.' . . . 'Bleed on, bleed on, soul, because I shall not cease to knife you until you are white and dry.' . . . 'Almost I tasted ecstasy and then came the Blare, and drowned perfection in perfection.' . . . 'I cannot endure it when I see you asleep, having carefully tucked your teddy bear beside you. I cannot endure it. Even if you would have been born anyhow. Even if you did choose me. Even if it was because I cannot endure it you chose me!' . . . 'Good nature, sweet nature and you'll have to be crushed. You shall not be; by God you shall not be. Whatever you do I will see that you are not crushed. I will not stand that you be crushed.' 'Feed the cat! feed the cat, you can't starve people though they can starve you. Might as well eat as I feed the cat; now the cat wants my food.' 'Consider and consider and always come back to what you saw in a flash and to what you knew when you saw it.' 'Give me power to choose to keep wisdom'. 'I will scald myself to cool.'

Yeats went on to quote:

> O sky harshen, O wind blow cold,
> O crags of stony thought be steep
> That mind may ache and bleed,
> That mind be scattered to the wind.
>
> All is true of all
> For all that is is true;
> But Truth is not;
> To become Truth
> Is not to be.
>
> Grief is not in Truth
> But Truth in grief must live grief
> Yet know no grief;
> For Truth is proof against all but itself.
>
> When all thought is gathered into the heart
> And set out to ripen like good fruit;
> And that which might have been eaten withered,
> And that which were better withered eaten;
> I sit and sit
> And marvel at the itch of it.
>
> I have counted all that may happen
> And it will not happen
> I have said all that shall be
> And it will not be.

O song, no tears but thine
Be sung, no thought
That is not secret
Shut out all others
For all earth must lie
But thou, and I.

While these quotations convey the general effect of 'Snatch-ings', a few additional observations may be worth making. The full title of the material was 'Moments. Snatchings – and Probings'. The theme of 'Snatchings' is illustrated by these ex-tracts:

God, you've made me laugh just when I thought
I should write a poem to shake the earth . . .
There you go again snatching things away . . .
I will not be defied by God, by men or by beast . . .
'Come along gentlemen',
Swallow, swallow,
Must drink up . . .
Rushing, crushing,
Howling at you . . .
No time to
Enjoy or watch –
Can't swallow, God, I'm sick . . .
Sober again; . . .
                    Always snatching, God.

This idea of frustration, which is echoed in her letters, blends with the idea of 'Moments', under which heading are short pieces, in prose and in verse, in which the theme that suffering is the way to change one's destiny recurs:

I have wedged this stripped, slithery hand in the machinery, that, through the impenetrable thrumming pain, one eager ravishing note shall dance to succour me . . .

Rain softens, rain, rain my tears on the parched earth of my heart,
There shall a flower open, there shall I tend and watch,
O rivers of the heart that run deep under the caked earth,
Do not put out one flame, rivers, because I want to see
One flower bud, blossom and die – UNCUT.

Mixed with these are unformed or half-formed jottings which convey the confusion of mind of a woman torn by problems of the relation of herself to God, of the daily drudgery and futility of life, of the care of her child, and of literary creativity. In one mood a postage stamp becomes a symbol of the order she hates, in another she prays to God to cherish those who love her and those she loves, or writes in desperation:

> One, two, three, one two three
> I can't count, I can't see;
> Break free, break free . . .
> Two three, two three.

This sense of being trapped is frequent.

Letter 59. 'Naked against thy breast I lie': unpublished.

Letters 61–2. Her poems mentioned in these letters were not published. 'Sweep on Doom where the phlegm phrase comes' may refer to 'Shape me to Eternal Damnation to rid me of the phlegm' alluded to by Yeats in his introduction to *The Lemon Tree*. They were of the type of which he wrote there:

these poems seemed to have lost form. . . It was not now a falling back into convention but an obsession by her own essential quality; passion followed passion with such rapidity that she had no time for deliberate choice; she seemed indifferent to scansion, even to syntax.

Three poems unmentioned in these letters but published in *O.B.M.V.* are 'The Child Compassion', 'Spirit, Silken Thread', and 'Take Away'. These are nos. 356–8 in *O.B.M.V.*, which was published on 19 November 1936 and contained seven of her poems. The *London Mercury* for July 1936 had already published six of these seven poems, omitting 'Spirit, Silken Thread'. Finally in 1937 appeared *The Lemon Tree*, which contained all the *O.B.M.V.* poems and thirteen others. Seven of these, together with extracts from 'Snatchings', have been presented here. The remaining six were entitled 'Essence', 'Construction', 'The Apple', 'As Day to Night', 'What Flower Truth' and 'I sang my Child to Sleep'.

The Lemon Tree was on the whole reviewed favourably in June and July 1937. The *Manchester Guardian* and *Time and Tide* agreed that the technical weakness of the poems, which seemed improvised, did not prevent an effect of visionary simplicity and exaltation. The *New England Weekly* thought that the author was 'too chaotic and impatient to succeed more than three or four times'. William Plomer in the *Spectator* remarked perceptively that the poems gave 'a rare sense of coming into contact with a naked soul, and I think that for some the contact must be embarrassing, like an accidental intrusion upon privacy'. Perhaps the most favourable review, which was unsigned, appeared in the *Irish Times* (14 June 1937); it compared Margot Ruddock to the great Italian mystics, and, oddly enough to Synge; it also selected for special mention 'The Apple':

> O apple life
> That swingeth where
> My hand can pluck
> Thee, poison fruit.
>
> I'll peel thee down
> Unto the core
> Imperishable,
> Absolute.

In praising this poem's feeling and restraint, the reviewer compared her work to the later poetry of T. S. Eliot, 'where only the restraint is present, the desire having been throttled before it was born', a judgement which seems likely to have been inspired by Yeats.

APPENDIX B

The most obvious examples are the reduction of 'Autumn, Crystal Eye' from nine stanzas to two, and the pruning of one stanza from 'O Holy Water' and from 'Love Song'. Whatever she may have learned from this kind of discipline was probably undermined by her attempts to render Shri Purohit Swami's songs into English. The Swami's English, Yeats complained, was much too florid: 'It is amusing to see his delighted astonishment', he wrote to Dorothy Wellesley from Majorca, 'when he discovers that he can call a goddess "this handsome girl," or even "a pretty girl." instead of a "maiden of surpassing loveliness."' Further, the Swami had a fatal facility, composing, as Margot Ruddock says in one of her letters, '52 poems of sheer *ecstasy* in a day'. These would have been in Hindi or in Urdu and, whatever their original merit (a question which caused some acrimony between Yeats and Chandra Bose in 1937), the three examples of his work in English included in the *O.B.M.V.* are not particularly impressive.

While Margot Ruddock's merits and limitations as a poet should now be sufficiently clear, a few examples of Yeats's emendations to some of her other poems may be of interest.

SAY THAT I LOVED, SOLDIER

Ruddock	*Yeats*
Say that I loved, soldier,	What if I loved, soldier,
And it be said	And it were said
I drowsed half life away	I drowsed half life away
In Love-bed.	In Love-bed.

And would have burned out	And would have burned all
The other half	The rest away
Had I not sought in grief	Had I not found grief
Love.	On a day.

WEEP NOT

Ruddock	*Yeats*
Weep not! beloved for the grey of tears	Weep not! beloved, for that rush of tears
Is like a liquid veil upon thine eyes.	Is like a liquid veil upon thine eyes.
There is another dawn to suffer sighs,	What matter if another dawn bring sighs
There is another day for fevered fears.	Another hostile day its press of fears.
Weep not! for weeping so thou can'st not see	Weep not, a weeping eye can never see
How little threads of comfort may be drawn	How great a web of comfort may be drawn
Out of another's heart into thine own.	Out of another heart into thine own
Nor how my own two hands stretch forth to thee.	Nor even my two hands stretched out to thee.
And if at Dawn the little threads should break	What if the dawn that web of comfort break,
Weep not again, beloved, for my sake.	Mock at the dawn, beloved, for my sake.

Lastly, here is another short manuscript poem and note, undated and without address, which she sent him, possibly in April 1936:

> O in a year this life will drink
> That courage from my own, I think,
> And quilted lassitude be spread
> And light glare on a shattered lid.

And in a year I shall not know
Whether my bed be eased or no
For Comfort's down or Fortune's spear,
I shall be fleshless in a year.

P.S. I don't like the comfort's down and fortune's spear line. This I wrote in the morning and finished in the pub and if you say it is wrong all over I shall scream and stamp on my new frock. You see what Shakespeare has brought me to.

I have just thought that you are like toothache, not *you* but you at me.

Yeats altered this poem in his own hand to read as follows:

O in a year this life will drink
The courage from my pot of ink
Limp in this lassitude lie spread,
Though daylight glare upon my bed.
In a year I shall not know
Whether my bed be soft or no.
I shall be fleshless in a year
Skull and crossbones all the wear.

Understandably, none of these three poems were ever published, but they do provide some further evidence of the different temperaments and approaches to poetry which are revealed in the letters.

APPENDIX C

A NOTE ON SOME OTHER RELEVANT LETTERS

Letters 7 *and* 8

Mr Harry Partch is now living at Encenitas, California, where in August 1969 he recalled with pleasure meeting Yeats, with whom he visited the Abbey Theatre. He also met AE, who reminded him laughingly that Yeats was tone-deaf. He showed me two brief letters from Yeats; one, postmarked 21 February 1935, apologised for his failure to meet Partch in London, owing to his illness. The other, written on 5 August 1936, regretted his inability to write a preface to Partch's book, *Genesis of a Music*. Partch was then in Los Angeles and did not see Yeats again. A closer connection between them might have proved fruitful; Partch's music, which recently has had a critical success in New York, has been much influenced by Chinese, Japanese and American Indian music. It is played on a variety of instruments of his own invention; including giant marimbas, large glass cloud-chamber bells, and xylophone-like instruments made from tubular sections of giant bamboos. His *Oedipus* has been recorded, with other of his compositions by Gate 5 Records, but the translation used is not that of Yeats, whose agent refused permission, although Yeats had personally given it and at least one unrecorded performance of his translation set to Partch's music had taken place.

Through Mr Partch's courtesy, xerox copies of Yeats's letters to him are now in the National Library of Ireland.

The only extant letter from Margot to Mrs Yeats is somewhat puzzling. It reads as follows:

133

Dear Mrs Yeats,
   Herewith the letter Yeats asked me to post to you to keep. I
picked him things to 'object' to through my solicitor, and would
have picked lots more but I don't want to do others out of their
'objections' we mustn't all object about the same things!
   I made it quite clear to my solicitor that whilst threatening such,
we none of us wanted a law case. I think a good stiff letter should
have effect. Yours sincerely,

                                                    Margot Collis

This letter may refer to some threatened legal action against
Ashley Dukes. On the other hand her letter of 4 May 1936
(no. 53) mentions her solicitor and it is possible that she misdated her letter to Mrs Yeats. If so, it might refer to a threatened
action against some newspaper. This possibility seems to be
ruled out by the first sentence, as it does not seem likely that
Yeats saw her in London in 1936. However, he could have sent
her the letter mentioned. It was not among the letters in Mrs
Yeats's file.

Yeats's letters to the Swami were sold by his daughter, Mrs
Chitale, to a dealer in Great Britain and were subsequently
bought privately by Mr Claude Driver, Director of the Rosen-
bach Foundation in Philadelphia, who informed me that they
are his personal property and are not available for inspection.
I understand that they mention Yeats's anxiety as to Margot
Ruddock's location late in 1937, and his subsequent distress
upon discovering that she had been committed; further that
they cast some light on Mrs Foden and her relationship with
the Swami. It is to be hoped that these letters will be made
available to interested scholars.

BIBLIOGRAPHY

Original Sources:

Yeats papers: Margot Ruddock's letters, poems by her in manuscript and typescript, her 'Adventures' and parts of his introduction to *The Lemon Tree*, in his handwriting.

Ruddock papers: letters from Yeats and Shri Purohit Swami; poems by her in manuscript and typescript, photographs, press cuttings.

Printed Sources:

Yeats, W. B.: *A Full Moon in March* (London, Macmillan, 1935).
Modern Poetry (London, B.B.C., 1936).
(ed.) *The Oxford Book of Modern Verse* (Oxford, Clarendon Press, 1936).
Yeats-Sturge Moore Correspondence (London, Routledge & Kegan Paul, 1953).
Collected Poems (London, Macmillan, 1961).
Collected Plays (London, Macmillan, 1963).

Ruddock, Margot: 'Poems: by Margot Ruddock with Prefatory Notes on the Author by W. B. Yeats', *London Mercury*, July 1936.
The Lemon Tree, with an introduction by W. B. Yeats (London, Dent, 1937).

Purohit Swami, Shri: *An Indian Monk* with introduction by W. B. Yeats (London, Macmillan, 1932).
The Song of Silence (Chitale, Poona City, no date).
The Holy Mountain by Bhagwān Shri Hamsa, translated by Shri Purohit Swami, introduction by W. B. Yeats (London, Faber & Faber, 1934).
– with W. B. Yeats: *The Ten Principal Upanishads* done into English (London, Faber & Faber, 1937).

Dasgupta, R. F. (ed.): *Rabindranath Tagore and W. B. Yeats* (University of Delhi, 1965): contains essays by Chandra Bose and others.

Fay, W. G.: *The Fays of the Abbey Theatre* (London, Rich & Cowan, 1935).

Fay, Gerard: *The Abbey Theatre, Cradle of Genius* (Dublin, Clonmore & Reynolds, 1958).

Hartnoll, Phyllis (ed.): *The Oxford Companion to the Theatre* (Oxford University Press, 1951).

Hone, Joseph: *W. B. Yeats, 1865–1939* (London, Macmillan, 1942).

Krause, David: *Sean O'Casey, the Man and his Work* (London, Macmillan, 1960).

Mokashi-Punekar, S.: *The Later Phase in the Development of W. B. Yeats* (Karnatak University, Dhawar, 1966).

O'Connor, Frank: *My Father's Son* (Dublin, Gill & Macmillan, 1968).

Robinson, Lennox (ed.): *Ireland's Abbey Theatre* (London, Sidgwick & Jackson, 1951).

Rothenstein, Sir William: *Since Fifty* (London, Faber & Faber, 1939).

Wade, Allan: *A Bibliography of the Writings of W. B. Yeats* (2nd edition, revised, London, Hart-Davis, 1958).

– (ed): *The Letters of W. B. Yeats* (London, Hart-Davis, 1954).

Wellesley, Dorothy: *Letters on Poetry from W. B. Yeats to Dorothy Wellesley* (Oxford University Press, 1940).

INDEX

Enfermeria Evangelica, 98
Epsom, 118
Evening News, 72
Evening Standard, 33, 72

Fay, Frank, 13, 50
Fay, Gerard, *The Abbey Theatre*, 50
Fay, W. G., 13, 50–1; *The Fays of the Abbey Theatre*, 50
Fearon, W. R., *Parnell of Avondale*, 20 n
Ferguson, Sir Samuel, *Congal*, 64
'Field, Michael', 68 and n, 69, 71
fleas, 87 and n
Foden, Mrs, 99 and n, 106, 111, 134
Frenz, Professor Horst, 8

Gaelic League, 46 n
Gagarin, Yuri, 63 n
Garnett, Richard, 8
George V, King, 72
Goethe, J. W. von, 80
Gogarty, Oliver St John, 11, 32
Gonne, Maud, 116
Goring, Marius, 52
Gregory, Lady, 116
Group Theatre, 11, 34 n
Groves, Olive, 117
Guthrie, Tyrone, 37, 38 and n, 40

Halliday, Simone, 8, 9, 12, 54, 56, 67, 77, 101, 113–14
Harding, M. V., 52
Henley, W. E., 36
Higgins, F. R., 28 n, 49 n; *Deuce of Jacks*, 28 n
Hone, Joseph, *W. B. Yeats*, 98, 117–118
Hopkins, Gerard Manley, 13, 39 and n
Hotel Terramar, 64, 67, 69, 74
Housman, A. E., *A Shropshire Lad*, 66 and n
Hsiung, S. I., *Lady Precious Stream*, 54

India, Indians, 11, 21, 82, 85, 93, 94, 100, 101, 104, 107, 117

Institute of Indian Mysticism, 11, 99 n
Iremonger, Valentin, 8
Irish Academy of Letters, 29, 43
Irish Times, 57 and n, 128
Isherwood, Christopher, 34 n

James, Henry, 36
Jane (old servant), 83
Jeffares, Professor A. Norman, 8
Job, 21 and n
Jo's Bar, 84
Joyce, James, 14
Joyce, Lucia, 14
Jung, C. G., 14

Kameny Theatre, 22
Kildare Street Club, 24, 31, 38
King's Hall, 52
Kingsley, Charles, 31 and n
Kipling, Rudyard, 36
Krause, David, *Sean O'Casey: The Man and his Work*, 43

Lagerkvist, Pår, *The Hangman*, 52, 55; *Bödeln*, 52
Langley, Noel, *For Ever*, 33 and n
Larchet, John, 57 n
Lawasha, 117
Leblanc, Georgette, 22, 23
Lindberg, Pår, *The Hangman*, 52
Linnebach, Adolf, 22
Little Theatre, 42, 55, 56, 65
Lomas, Herbert, 52
London Mercury, 102, 105 n, 111
London Stage Society, 52
Lovell, Raymond, 9 and n, 27, 33, 41, 47, 53, 67, 68, 72, 73, 77, 86–7, 98, 99, 101, 102, 106, 111, 112, 113

MacKenna, Stephen, 45 and n
Macmanus, Captain Dermot, 32 n
Macmillan & Co., 29, 34
MacNamara, Brinsley, 43–4, 48–9, 49 n; *The Valley of Squinting Windows*, 43
MacNeice, Louis, 34 n

138

back', 30; 'The Old Men Admiring Themselves in the Water', 30, 110; 'Running to Paradise', 31; 'Supernatural Songs', 10, 11; 'Sweet Dancer', 14, 116, 119; 'To Dorothy Wellesley', 116; 'What lively lad most pleasured me', 30

Yeats, Mrs W. B., 12, 22, 26, 32, 36, 43, 46, 72–4, 79, 93, 98, 99, 117, 133–4

'Yeats Festival', 52, 54